Sarah Kane's *4.48 Psychosis*

T0383986

'Everything passes/Everything perishes/Everything palls'
4.48 Psychosis

How on earth do you award aesthetic points to a 75-minute suicide note? The question comes from a review of *4.48 Psychosis'*
inaugural production, staged the year after Sarah Kane took her
own life, but this book explores the ways in which it misses the
point. Instead, Kane's final play is much more than a bizarre fare-
well to mortality. It's a work best understood by approaching it
first and foremost as theatre – as a singular component in a theatrical assemblage of bodies, voices, light and energy. The play finds
an unexpectedly close fit in the established traditions of modern
drama and the practices of postdramatic theatre.

Glenn D'Cruz explores this theatrical angle through a number of exemplary professional and student productions with a
focus on the staging of the play by the Belarus Free Theatre
(2005) and Melbourne's Red Stitch Theatre (2007).

Glenn D'Cruz teaches drama and cultural studies at Deakin
University, Australia.

The Fourth Wall

The Fourth Wall series is a growing collection of short books on famous plays. Its compact format perfectly suits the kind of fresh, engaging criticism that brings a play to life.

Each book in this series selects one play or musical as its subject and approaches it from an original angle, seeking to shed light on an old favourite or break new ground on a modern classic. These lively, digestible books are a must for anyone looking for new ideas on the major works of modern theatre.

www.routledge.com/performance/series/4THW

Also available in this series:

J. M. Synge's *The Playboy of the Western World* by Christopher Collins
Heiner Müller's *The Hamletmachine* by David Barnett
Lerner and Loewe's *My Fair Lady* by Keith Garebian
Samuel Beckett's *Krapp's Last Tape* by Daniel Sack
Thornton Wilder's *The Skin of Our Teeth* by Kyle Gillette
Harold Pinter's *Party Time* by Graham White
Davies and Penhall's *Sunny Afternoon* by John Fleming
Tim Crouch's *An Oak Tree* by Catherine Love
Sondheim and Lapine's *Into the Woods* by Olaf Jubin
Errol John's *Moon on a Rainbow Shawl* by Lynnette Goddard

Coming soon:

George Büchner's *Woyzeck* by Karoline Gritzner
Benjamin Britten's *Peter Grimes* by Sam Kinchin-Smith
J. M. Barrie's *Peter Pan* by Lucie Sutherland
Sondheim and Wheeler's *Sweeney Todd* by Aaron Thomas
Caryl Churchill's *Far Away* by Dan Rebellato
August Wilson's *Joe Turner's Come and Gone* by Ladrica Menson-Furr
Alastair McDowell's *Pomona* by David Ian Rabey
Rogers and Hammerstein's *The Sound of Music* by Julian Woolford

Sarah Kane's
4.48 Psychosis

Glenn D'Cruz

Routledge
Taylor & Francis Group

LONDON AND NEW YORK

First published 2018
by Routledge
2 Park Square, Milton Park, Abingdon, Oxon OX14 4RN

and by Routledge
711 Third Avenue, New York, NY 10017

Routledge is an imprint of the Taylor & Francis Group, an informa business

© 2018 Glenn D'Cruz

British Library Cataloguing-in-Publication Data
A catalogue record for this book is available from the British Library

Library of Congress Cataloguing-in-Publication Data
A catalog record for this book has been requested

ISBN: 978-1-138-09747-6 (pbk)
ISBN: 978-1-315-10485-0 (ebk)

Typeset in Bembo
by Out of House Publishing

For Lenny and Sonia

Contents

Figures

Acknowledgements

Thanks to my students, especially those who performed in my production of *4.48 Psychosis* at Deakin University in 2007. To Alyson Campbell for sharing her experience of directing the play for Melbourne's Red Stitch Theatre Company. To Vladimir Shcherban, Sasha Padziarei and Nikolai Khalezin for their contributions to my chapter on the Belarus Free Theatre's productions of the play. To Ben Piggott for his encouragement and editorial wisdom. And, finally, to Leonard D'Cruz for his editing and critical comments.

Note: all in-text references refer to the Methuen edition of *4.48 Psychosis* published in *Sarah Kane Complete Plays* (2001) London: Methuen.

Contextualising
4.48 Psychosis

'Everybody loves a dead girl' – Sarah Kane as innovator and icon

4.48 Psychosis is an unusual play. On the page, it looks more like an experimental poem than a conventional theatre script. It is divided into 24 segments (rather than acts and scenes). Some are lucid, others abstract and a few are just plain confounding. There are few logical connections between these fragments beyond thematic references to depression, suicide and various clinical practices used to treat mental illness. There is no plot, and the text doesn't specify a setting or delineate distinct characters, although it is possible to occasionally infer such things (in the voices of lovers, friends, doctors and patients distributed throughout the work). The play's author, Sarah Kane, said *4.48 Psychosis* is about:

> a psychotic breakdown and what happens to a person's mind when the barriers which distinguish between reality and different forms of imagination completely disappear, so that you no longer know the difference between your waking life and your dream life. And also you no longer know where you stop and the world starts.
>
> (Quoted in Saunders, 2009, 81)

This account of the play partially explains its unconventional form. Perhaps Kane believed the experience of clinical depression is best conveyed through fragments that favour metaphor over literal description and conventional narrative. The play's unusual structure poses several challenges for those interested in staging the work. Should it be performed as a monologue, or is it more suited to an ensemble of actors? How should the director allocate lines? How should actors intone Kane's words? Is the play more effective when the performers rant or rave, or is a sober style of delivery more effective? Is it important to set the play in a particular location, or does a more abstract setting heighten the work's potential to engender a visceral response from its audiences? That the play generates such questions accounts for why it has inspired so many diverse and compelling productions. In my view, the play works much better on the stage than the page, which is why this short book devotes so much space to the play in performance.

4.48 Psychosis is also shrouded in mythology. At the age of 28, on the 20 February 1999, Sarah Kane committed suicide in King's College Hospital, London, thereby ensuring that the circumstances of her untimely death will forever haunt her legacy as a playwright. 'How on earth do you award aesthetic points to a 75-minute suicide note?' wrote Michael Billington in his review of the play's inaugural production staged a year after Kane's death (2001). Some critics argue that approaching the play as autobiography detracts from its value as a work of art (Roberts, 2015; Diedrich, 2013). Kane's brother famously issued a press statement pointing out that while the play is about suicidal despair, it's 'not a thinly veiled suicide note' (Sierz, 2000, 90). Kane's reputation as a merchant of doom preceded

4.48 Psychosis. Regarding her earlier play, *Cleansed*, Charles Spencer observed that 'you feel her work owes much more to clinical depression than to real artistic vision' (1998). Kane countered such caricatures of her work, declaring that

> I don't find my plays depressing or lacking in hope. But then I am someone whose favourite band is Joy Division because I find their songs uplifting. To create something beautiful about despair, or out of a feeling of despair, is for me the most hopeful, life-affirming thing a person can do.
>
> (Quoted in Sierz, 2000, 91)

The question of whether Kane's plays are life-affirming or not is almost beside the point considering her posthumous status as a tragic icon, a fate bestowed on so many artists who die young: Sylvia Plath, Arthur Rimbaud, John Keats, Percy Bysshe Shelley, Ian Curtis, and the members of the 27 club such as Jimi Hendrix, Janis Joplin, Jim Morrison, Kurt Cobain and Amy Winehouse. Kane may have missed joining this exclusive group by a slim margin, but an aura of despair and tragedy clings to her posthumous reputation. Kane's agent, Mel Kenyon, recalled that someone once remarked that 'everybody loves a dead girl, especially if she was talented' (quoted in Saunders, 2002, 144). While there is much more to Kane's life and art than the manner of her death, there is little point in evading the fact that her suicide and celebrity status shapes the way people approach her work.

Annabelle Singer observed that there were two broad schools of thought regarding Kane after her demise: 'one saw her entire body of work in light of her suicide, the other mourned her death, but declined to even try to connect her death and her work' (Singer, 2004, 160). There are risks associated with adopting a narrowly autobiographical approach to *4.48 Psychosis*, but there are also problems with espousing an overly formalistic approach to the text that ignores the fact that it was Kane's personal experience of being treated for a mental illness that 'formed the material' for the play, 'which is perhaps uniquely painful for the reader in that it appears to have been written in the almost certain knowledge that it would be performed posthumously' (Greig, 2001, xv). In short, the former position produces a romantic deification of the author, while the latter underestimates the relationship between personal experience and creative expression.

In his seminal essay, 'The Death of the Author', Roland Barthes argued that there is no compelling reason to assume that the author of a work is the ultimate guarantor of meaning. Indeed, this belief, in Barthes' view, restricts the richness of writing by closing down interpretative possibilities and ignoring the fact that a text is 'a multi-dimensional space in which a variety of writings, none of them original, blend and clash. The text is a tissue of quotations drawn from the innumerable centres of culture' (1977, 146). As we shall see, *4.48 Psychosis* provides an exemplary illustration of Barthes' thesis, for Kane weaves together a dizzying array of quotations from a wide range of sources – from the run-out groove inscription on a Joy Division record to extracts from biblical scriptures to excerpts from medical textbooks. The welter of references and quotations in the play partially accounts for its dramaturgical malleability in performance. In short, the play, as David Greig astutely notes, presents a fragmented mind 'which is the author, and which is more than the author' (2001, xvii).

Affective aesthetics

To say the play has nothing to do with Kane's suicide seems imprudent, but dwelling on its autobiographical elements delimits its considerable value as a play. Mark Ravenhill, one of Kane's contemporaries, wrote that 'Myth, biography and gossip crowd around the work of any artist, clouding our view, but maybe no one more so at the moment than Sarah Kane. We don't know her. We never knew her. Let's look at her work' (Ravenhill, 2005). Like all plays, *4.48 Psychosis* leads a double life: one on the page, the other on stage. The problem with Ravenhill's imperative is that when we look at Kane's work in performance, we are also watching the work of actors, directors, designers and technicians. This book is primarily concerned with the play in performance because I believe the key to understanding Kane's work lies in her exploration of the affective possibilities of performance. She once remarked:

> Increasingly, I'm finding performance much more inter-esting than acting; theatre more compelling than plays. Unusually for me, I'm encouraging my friends to see my play *Crave* before reading it, because I think of it more as a text for performance than as a play. The sexual conno-tations of 'performance' are not coincidental. Liverpool's [soccer player] Paul Ince publicly admits that he finds tackling more enjoyable than sex. Performance is visceral.

As we can see from this quotation (1998, 12), Sarah Kane liked football. She also enjoyed music. More specifically, she was a fan of Manchester United, and Joy Division. I mention these autobiographical facts because they convey something important about Kane's artistic ambitions, and if you want to understand why so many people continue to stage *4.48 Psychosis* and celebrate its considerable innovations, it's important to note that Kane wanted her plays to generate something akin to the visceral experience of attending a football match or a rock concert: 'I frequently walk out of the theatre early without fear of missing anything. But however bad I've felt, I've never left a football match early, because you never know when a miracle might occur' (Kane, 1998, 12). She also lamented the fact that theatre rarely creates the affective intensity produced by music, pointing out – with reference to attending a concert by The Jesus and Mary Chain – that music often directly connects with the experience of its audience in a way that often eludes the theatre: 'It [music] puts you in direct physical contact with thought and feeling' (1998, 12). Let's pause here and unpack these statements.

What has football and rock music got to do with the theatre? And why am I writing about sport and music in a book about *4.48 Psychosis*? First, if you're not a football fan, or if you've never attended a rock concert by the likes of, say, Patti Smith, or Nick Cave and the Bad Seeds, it's going to be difficult to make sense of Kane's enthusiasm for these events. The experience of attending a sporting event or concert, for those with an emotional investment in these spectacles, is a *physical* experience. At their best, sport and music can invoke a Dionysian energy that produces a palpable bond between performers and spectators. This is not to say that such a relationship is unique to these performance events; in theory, any invested contemplation can produce visceral sensations – that's one of the reasons people weep at the cinema, for example. We possess the ability to be emotionally affected by two-dimensional representations on the silver screen, and much else besides. However, we often apprehend the spontaneous overflow of powerful feelings in sporting arenas and concert halls, where audiences vicariously participate in sublime feats of athletic and aesthetic prowess. As a fan of these popular entertainments myself, I know what Kane means when she observed that 'there are some wonderful performances in Edinburgh … but there is only one David Beckham' (Kane, 1998, 12).

I don't fully understand Kane's enthusiasm for Beckham since I've spent most of my adult life in Melbourne, Australia (I'm assuming 'Becks' was a fair footballer!). I am, however, a fan of Australian Rules Football (AFL), which, like the so-called 'world game' has an aesthetic appeal which is eminently theatrical. Two teams engage in hostile combat, which generates dramatic tension; the spectators witness sudden changes of momentum, tragic reversals of fortune; the game has its heroes and villains, and it's foolish to predict the outcome of the contest in advance, for you never know when an underdog is going to become feral and take a massive bite out of a champion's backside. What's not to like? At the risk of sounding like a proselytising maniac, I'm going to give you a short account of what Ric Knowles calls kinaesthetic empathy – that is, the physical sensation that makes the spectator feel as though they're playing the game themselves (2017, 26). Now, some people would have you believe that live performance is especially good at facilitating such a kinaesthetic exchange between performer and spectator. I take Philip Auslander's point that there are no convincing grounds for claiming that live events are defined by enabling a transfer of energy from performer to spectator and back again in a feedback loop. In fact, he dismisses attempts to celebrate the co-presence of actors and spectators in the theatre as mystification (1999, 2). Put another way, he argues that there is no absolute distinction between theatre and media: all mediums can trigger emotional and kinetic sensations in spectators. So, I proffer a televised AFL match as an example of what I am calling, after Knowles, kinaesthetic exchange.

It's 13 August 2016. My team, the West Coast Eagles, look like they're about to be knocked out of the finals race (which is something akin to the NFL playoffs). For the last two minutes, the Eagles have been locked in a fierce goal-for-goal contest against the GWS Giants. I can feel my heart racing, and beads of sweat cling to my clammy skin; I feel exhausted, my hands are shaking, and my knees are weak; I'm not in love, but, as the old Elvis song says, I'm all shook up. I watch the clock tick down to 54 seconds on my TV screen, and I can see the opposition supporters celebrating their anticipated victory. Surely, it's all over. I'm now slumped on my couch; I feel tightness in my chest – even though I'm resigned to my team's impending demise, the palpitations won't let up. Then, a minor miracle – my favourite player, Nic Naitanui, somehow breaks away from his opponent and snaps a kick towards goal, and my right leg involuntarily mirrors the champion's kicking motion. I scream like a banshee from hell as the ball sails through the big sticks just as time expires. I collapse in a heap on my lounge room floor exhausted, spent and elated. This is not the sort of behaviour one sees in the theatre on a regular basis, yet this is precisely the kind of visceral response Kane hoped to generate through her work.

The salient point is that, for the committed fan, football – whether experienced as a live event or a broadcast – produces powerful, visceral affects through the display of rigorous athletic *performance*. Kane found the performative dimension of theatre the most compelling thing about the medium, and I suspect her enthusiasm for football and music was partially the result of her finding a resonance between these mediums and certain kinds of theatrical performance. Of course, Kane was by no means the first person to make the connection between sport and theatre, or attempt to conceive of theatre as a primarily affective medium, and in any case, we can only stretch the analogy between sport and theatre so far. But as a drama student, Kane was well versed in the theories of Antonin Artaud and the principles he espoused in his writings about performance and the so-called theatre of cruelty. Consider this quotation from Artaud's *Manifesto in Clear Language*: 'I destroy because for me everything that proceeds from reason is untrustworthy. I believe only in the evidence of what stirs my marrow, not in the evidence of what addresses itself to my reason. I have found levels in the realm of the nerve' (1988, 108). Here, Artaud not only identifies sensory experience as being superior to reason, but claims that the *evidence* of the senses – 'what stirs the marrow' – is a form of knowledge:

> The eternal conflict between reason and the heart is decided in my very flesh, but in my flesh irrigated by nerves. In the realm of the affective imponderable, the image provided by my nerves takes the form of the highest intellectuality, which I refuse to strip of its quality of intellectuality.

Before leaving the resonances between sport and theatre behind, we should acknowledge the influence of Bertolt Brecht's ideas about spectatorship on the formation of Kane's aesthetic preferences. Brecht called for a 'smoker's theatre', which encouraged spectators 'to puff away at its cigars as if watching a boxing match' (Brecht, 1978, 8). Health and safety regulations have consigned Brecht's metaphor to the dustbin of history; it's no longer possible to smoke at a boxing match, or any other sporting event, for good reason, but his general observation about the engaged sports fan remains compelling. Contesting decisions made by a referee or umpire is an integral part of watching sport, and it's crucially, for Brecht, part of the *fun* of being invested in sport. Indeed, he consistently argued that the German theatre of his time took itself too seriously, and consequently bored the pants off its audience because there was no 'sport' in the institution (1978, 9). It would be disingenuous to claim that Kane's theatre is a barrel of laughs – a play like *4.48 Psychosis* is not devoid of a certain kind of black humour, as we shall discover, but it's not *fun* in Brecht's sense of the term. However, it can be as compelling as sport under the right circumstances.

As much as she loved football, Sarah Kane was also passionate about art. It's important to stress that a wide range of performance practices informed her work as a dramatist. She cites an exhibition she attended by Mona Hatoum at the Scottish Gallery of Modern Art as being particularly absorbing (1998, 12):

> In a tiny cylindrical room I watched a projection of a surgical camera disappearing into every orifice of the artist. True, few people could stay in the room as long as me, but I found the voyage up Mona Hatoum's arse put me in powerful and direct contact with my feelings about my own mortality. I can't ask for much more.

Several of Kane's critics and commentators take her observation that 'performance is visceral' as their point of departure for explaining the power of her writing (Campbell, 2005;

Saunders, 2002). Most of these critics qualify their commentary by acknowledging that it's impossible to prove that any piece of writing or performance is inherently capable of generating visceral affects in the bodies of spectators. Put simply, what turns me on might leave you cold, depending on an almost limitless set of variables (such as aesthetic prejudices, political dispositions, moods, temperaments and whatever intoxicating substance any given spectator might have imbibed before witnessing any given performance).

Context: 'Cool Britannia' and in-yer-face theatre

I will conclude this introduction with a few brief remarks about the play's social and political context. Kane belonged to a generation of playwrights who first made their mark in the mid-to-late 1990s in the UK. This group includes writers such as Anthony Neilson, Jez Butterworth, Irvine Welch and Mark Ravenhill. Aleks Sierz (2000, 5) coined the term 'In-Yer-Face Theatre' to articulate themes and stylistic characteristics shared by this generation of playwrights.

> How can you tell if a play is in-yer-face? It really isn't difficult: the language is usually filthy, characters talk about unmentionable subjects, take their clothes off, have sex, humiliate each other, experience unpleasant emotions, become suddenly violent. At its best, this kind of theatre is so powerful, so visceral, that it forces audiences to react.

In short, the writers that Sierz groups together under his rather awkward moniker produced provocative and confrontational work that apparently embraced new political possibilities that opened up in the wake of the fall of communism and the end of conservative rule in the UK. Sierz also provides an account of how small theatres such as the Bush – under the artistic directorship of Dominic Dromgoole – nurtured new writing before older institutions like the Royal Court staged plays by Kane and her contemporaries. Today, we remember the UK in the 1990s as an era marked by the rise of Tony Blair's New Labour, Britpop, and the so-called Young British Artists (YBA) who included Tracey Emin and Damien Hirst. Their work in the visual arts was as confrontational and provocative as their counterparts in the theatre world. While there is little doubt that the tenor of the times influenced Kane's writing to some extent, one of the most remarkable things about *4.48 Psychosis* is that it doesn't read like a play that's almost twenty years old. This is not to say that it embodies universal values or conveys some definitive truth about mental illness. Rather, the play's continuing popularity is a testament to Kane's talent as a playwright. A lot of people suffer from mental illness, but few manage to find a way to convey the details of their experience in art.

In this book, I'm going to adopt a very pragmatic standpoint, and unpack the complexities of the play from the perspective of someone who teaches it as drama, but has also directed the play with students, and grappled with trying to bring this unusual text to life. I'm interested in what you can do with the play practically, and what it discloses about the world, and the oppositions that divide people into rigid identities: black, white, brown, male, female, mad, sane and so on. To achieve this latter aim, it's necessary to look at how other people have read and performed the play. However, in keeping with Kane's enthusiasm for performance, I will focus on productions of the play I have either seen directly or witnessed on video and engage with the creative processes of those responsible for directing these works.

In Chapter 2, I will focus on the play's themes, and identify the ways they are articulated through Kane's formal innovations. I will frame this discussion by engaging with trauma theory and the concept of postdramatic theatre. In Chapter 3, I will provide a detailed reading of the play with a focus on its points of resonance with postdramatic theatre. Chapter 4 will explore some of the key practical and ethical problems generated by teaching *4.48 Psychosis* in the context of a university production I directed in 2007. Chapter 5 will focus on three professional productions of the play: Alyson Campbell's version for Melbourne's Red Stitch Company and the Belarus Free Theatre's landmark staging in 2005 and its restaging in London in 2015. This chapter will also include a list of other noteworthy productions of the play. I will conclude the book by locating the play within a wider intellectual tradition, arguably inaugurated by Michel Foucault's book, *Madness and Civilization: A History of Insanity in the Age of Reason* (1964), and interrogate the way the play unsettles the borders that separate madness from reason.

References

Artaud, Antonin (1988) *Antonin Artaud: Selected Writings*. Translated by Farrar, Straus and Giroux. Berkeley, CA and Los Angeles, CA: University of California Press.

Auslander, Philip (1999) *Liveness: Performance in a Mediatized Culture*. London and New York: Routledge.

Badiou, Alain (2005) *Handbook of Inaesthetics*. Translated by Alberto Toscano. Stanford, CA: Stanford University Press.

Barthes, Roland (1977) 'The Death of the Author'. *Image-Music-Text*. Translated by Stephen Heath. London: Fontana Press.

Billington, Michael (2000) 'How do you Judge a 75-Minute Suicide Note?' *The Guardian* www.theguardian.com/stage/2000/jun/30/theatre.artsfeatures. Accessed 27 July 2017.

Brecht, Bertolt (1978) *Brecht on Theatre: The Development of an Aesthetic*. Edited and translated by John Willett. New York: Hill and Wang.

Campbell, Alyson (2005) 'Experiencing Kane: an Affective Analysis of Sarah Kane's "Experiential" Theatre in Performance'. *Australasian Drama Studies* 46: 80–97.

Diedrich, Antje (2013) '"Last in a Long Line of Literary Kleptomaniacs": Intertextuality in Sarah Kane's *4.48 Psychosis*'. *Modern Drama* 56:3: 374–398.

Foucault, Michel (1964) *Madness and Civilization: A History of Insanity in the Age of Reason*. New York: Pantheon Books.

Greig, David (2001) 'Introduction'. *Sarah Kane: Complete Plays*. London: Methuen.

Kane, Sarah (1998) 'Why can't theatre be as gripping as footie?' *The Guardian* www.theguardian.com/stage/2015/jan/12/sarah-kane-theatre-football-blasted. Accessed 27 July 2017.

Knowles, Ric (2017) 'A Pedagogical Trip to the Field of Dreams'. *Canadian Theatre Review* 169:Winter: 26–29.

Lehmann, Hans-Thies (2006) *Postdramatic Theatre*. Translated and with an afterword by Karen Jürs-Munby. London and New York: Routledge.

Ravenhill, Mark (2005) 'Suicide Art? She's Better than That'. *The Guardian* www.theguardian.com/stage/2005/oct/12/theatre. Accessed 27 July 2017.

Roberts, Matthew (2015) 'Vanishing Acts: Sarah Kane's Texts for Performance and Postdramatic Theatre'. *Modern Drama* 58:1: 94–111.

Saunders, Graham (2002) *Love Me or Kill Me: Sarah Kane and the Theatre of Extremes*. Manchester: Manchester University Press.

Saunders, Graham (2009) *About Kane: the Playwright and the Work*. London: Faber and Faber.

Sierz, Aleks (2000) *In-Yer-Face Theatre: British Drama Today*. London: Faber and Faber.

Singer, Annabelle (2004) Annabelle Singer, 'Don't Want to Be This: the Elusive Sarah Kane'. *The Drama Review* XLVIII:2: 139–171.

Spencer, Charles (1998) 'Severed limbs don't make you cutting-edge'. *The Telegraph* www.telegraph.co.uk/culture/4713653/Severed-limbs-dont-make-you-cutting-edge.html. Accessed 27 July 2017.

2

Reading *4.48 Psychosis*

The flaw in love (and psychiatry)

In the last chapter, I stated that this book would focus on *4.48 Psychosis* from the perspective of someone primarily interested in theatre practice. However, if you want to stage the play, you must read and interpret the text closely. Of course, this imperative applies to any dramatic text, but the 'open' structure of *4.48 Psychosis* requires any would-be director to make decisions about the size of the cast, the distribution of lines and the setting. Most plays include such details, but Kane's work demands that the director or creative ensemble fill in the blanks. Should you perform the play as a monologue, a two-hander, or use a large group of performers? Should you attempt to create characters that represent doctors and patients and distribute lines accordingly? Should you locate the play in a hospital or some other medical institution? Perhaps it might be more effective to take an abstract approach and situate the work in an indeterminate space? A close reading of the play will help you formulate a practical approach to solving these staging problems. But like all great works of art, Kane's play is about many things, and no single reading or production can provide a definitive account of what it means. However, most readers will notice that certain themes recur throughout the text. In this chapter, I will discuss *4.48 Psychosis* under two broad headings, 'love' and 'psychiatry', since they will enable me to unpack two of the work's most insistent topics.

Attempting to articulate the experience of mental illness is a daunting prospect when there is no absolute consensus about its causes and treatment. Why do pharmacological drugs work for some people and not others? Why are some people more predisposed to this type of illness than others? What role do behavioural, cultural and environmental factors play in the disease? Of course, medical specialists formulate theories about the causes of mental illness, and, as we shall see, Kane contests the validity of some of these explanations. Experts from the fields of psychoanalysis, philosophy and psychiatry, among many, also proffer ideas about why people suffer from depression and anxiety. In explicating *4.48 Psychosis*, I will, where appropriate, make references to some of these expert opinions about the causes of mental illness. However, it is important to remember that my primary concern is to identify what the play tells us about the phenomenon. Perhaps the poetic qualities of *4.48 Psychosis* convey something about the anguish of mental illness that eludes more direct and logical forms of expression. Andrew Solomon supports this idea when he writes that 'depression is grief out of proportion to circumstance. It is tumbleweed distress that thrives on thin air, growing despite its detachment from the nourishing earth. It can be described only in metaphor and allegory' (2014, 15). In short, mental illness is a complex phenomenon, and there is no simple approach to its diagnosis or treatment. I have no medical expertise, so I do not intend to provide a summary of the current state of scientific knowledge about the subject or offer any definitive judgment about the treatment of the malady.

I have never suffered from clinical depression. That is not to say I have never felt intimations of despair, but I write as someone who has not experienced significant trauma, or, perhaps more correctly, not *yet* experienced those forms of distress that precipitate an enduring dissolution of identity and personality. For to be human is to be vulnerable to contingent events that may shatter one's sense of self. We all live under the sign of precarity, but some people, more than others, experience a profound sense of sadness when they contemplate existential questions about mortality, the futility of being, or the value of life itself. Others find it difficult to locate and name the source of their exhausting anxiety and find existence an unbearable burden. Most of us, though, at some point in our lives will experience the devastating effects of love gone wrong. As Kane's favourite songwriter Ian Curtis once sang, love will tear us apart. And if we are particularly unlucky, love will tear us apart again (and again). Love features as a persistent theme in *4.48 Psychosis.* Most people eventually recover from the grief generated by a failed relationship, but others are not so lucky.

A psychoanalytic account of depression: mourning and melancholia

Have you ever tried to describe your feelings when love goes wrong? Have you ever tried to express the sensations you feel when you realise your lover has left you bereft with only your thoughts for company? It isn't easy to give grief an aesthetic form, which is why we heap praise on those people, like Sarah Kane, who find a way to transform personal pain into art. While relatively few people make insightful observations about the trauma generated by lost love, the general contours of the experience manifest as common symptoms. The familiar becomes strange, and a source of anxiety: the mere sight of a coffee cup once used by your lost love can trigger a torrent of tears; the strains of a familiar melody might precipitate an emotional meltdown. You might begin to hate yourself and compile a list of your flaws; flaws that prove that you are unworthy of anyone's affection. You might obsessively listen to torch songs, or, then again, you may just collapse in a heap and cry yourself to sleep.

In the immediate aftermath of a particularly traumatic relationship, I felt broken. It was as though some sharp object entered my body, and cut me up from the inside. How to numb this persistent ache? I recall collapsing onto the cold hardwood floor of my flat one evening after rapidly consuming a small bottle of whiskey, which failed to quell my anxiety and self-loathing. There I remained until a survival instinct kicked in and forced me to resume my everyday routine. I staggered through my days in a trance, like some automaton. In rare moments of clarity, I could feel my heart palpitating irregularly and my pulse beating unsteadily; embryonic tears often impaired my vision, I bloodied my nose on transparent glass on several occasions, for my eyes couldn't focus properly. I saw the world through broken glass; my flat, which I once shared with my lost love, took on the qualities of a portentous penitentiary – I could barely tolerate living there, and took every opportunity to avoid staying at home.

After a while, I found balance, an equilibrium of sorts, and even though I eventually fell in step with the rhythms of everyday life, I sensed an irreparable damage within. Sometimes, mostly when I lay alone in the bed I once shared with my ex-girlfriend, I felt as though I'd lost some essential part of my self. Several months passed, and this all-consuming ache receded.

Eventually, after a year or so, I felt as though life had returned to a stable state. I re-entered the world. This experience of mental trauma is not unusual, and I suspect most people at one time or another have gone through something similar. I recovered from this particular encounter with despair fairly quickly, but not everyone is as fortunate, and *4.48 Psychosis* is not about people who manage to pull out of a tailspin. An event like the one I have just described can precipitate a form of self-loathing that turns into depression. The experience of loss often precipitates this form of self-loathing. Freud made a distinction between mourning and melancholia, which Alicia Tycer uses to provide a psychoanalytic account of the kind of grief addressed in Kane's play. She reminds us that Freud believed that 'mourning is a reaction to a definable loss. Eventually, it can be overcome, but melancholia remains indefinitely' (2008, 25). In other words, mourning describes a process whereby one recovers from loss because it's possible to identify the source of one's pain. In my 'love gone wrong' anecdote, I identified my former girlfriend as the source of my pain and managed to distance myself from the trauma generated by our break-up. Depression emerges as a consequence of not being able to let go of the lost lover. According to Freud's theory, melancholia is a pathological condition that is a result of 'an identification of the ego with the abandoned object' (Freud, [1917] 1957 244). In other words, the person suffering from melancholia internalises the lost 'object' in a form that remains elusive and unidentifiable.

Consequently, the melancholic individual 'cannot define or become conscious of what has been lost, leading to an inability to achieve closure' (Tycer, 2008, 25). An all-consuming sadness pervades every aspect of life. Tycer provides a compelling account of how *4.48 Psychosis* resonates with psychoanalysis, and I will return to some of her insights in my discussion of the play's formal aesthetic qualities, but it is important not to lose sight of the fact that there are a bewildering number of theories about what causes depression. As William Styron notes, the 'very number of hypotheses is testimony to the malady's all but impenetrable mystery' (1992, 77). In any case, the play does not proffer any theory about the causes of depression but rather presents the experience of suffering from depression. It does, however, resonate strongly with the practice of self-loathing that is an essential feature of the psychoanalytic account of melancholia – it is worth remembering that the 'I' of the play is diagnosed with 'pathological grief' (223). However, violence directed at the self is only one of the play's central motifs.

An existential account of depression: love as anxiety

I now want to focus on the connections between mortality, loss and love from a different philosophical perspective. After cataloguing various states of being – 'I am sad', 'I feel that the future is hopeless and that things cannot improve', 'I am fat' (206), and listing a series of things the 'I' of the play cannot do – 'I can't think' 'I cannot make love', 'I cannot fuck' (207) – Kane writes: 'I have become so depressed by the fact of my mortality that I have decided to commit suicide' (207).

Why would the realisation that you are *mortal* make you want to hasten your death? Why should the fact of impermanence necessarily render life meaningless? These questions are irrelevant if you believe in life after death, but consciousness of mortality for those without religious beliefs can be unsettling. For Martin Heidegger – or at least the Heidegger of

Being and Time – mortality functions as the motor of human activity insofar as an awareness of our mortality – our 'being-towards-death' – is what makes life precious (1962). In other words, the ticking of the clock compels us to live authentically. That is, being-toward-death forces us to ignore the world's multiple distractions and trivial pursuits and focus on realising our potentialities. Kane may or may not have been conversant with Heidegger's philosophy, but she was certainly acquainted with the ideas of other existentialist thinkers if only as a keen student of Samuel Beckett. For many years, critics read Beckett's work within the framework of the so-called theatre of the absurd. Martin Esslin coined this phrase to describe the resonances between existential philosophy (especially in Albert Camus' account of the Absurd) and the work of playwrights such as Beckett, Ionesco and Adamov (2004). Indeed, Albert Camus' Absurdist philosophy provides an important point of resonance with Kane's play given that Camus identifies suicide as the primary question of philosophy. *The Myth of Sisyphus* famously opens with this provocative statement (1979, 11):

> There is but one truly significant philosophical problem, and that is suicide. Judging whether life is or is not worth living amounts to answering the fundamental question of philosophy. All the rest – whether or not the world has three dimensions, whether the mind has nine or twelve categories – comes afterwards. These are games; one must first answer.

This brief account of Camus' philosophy is all very well, but it does not explain why the play contends that 'the fact of mortality' (Kane, 2001, 207) is the source of despair, and spur to suicide. I think it's only possible to understand the weight of this phrase if we connect the play's anxiety about mortality to the experience of love as a source of terror. In short, mortality is love's primary condition of possibility. We can only value the life of another person because it is finite. If our loved ones were immortal, we would have nothing to lose, so they would not be precious. The key point here is that loss, or the fear of losing someone, or something, is at the heart of the play. At best – if your lover doesn't leave you for another, or decides to leave you because they can no longer tolerate you – they will eventually die, and you will find yourself alone and forsaken unless, of course, you die first, and are, therefore, spared the pain of loss.

> Cut out my tongue
> Tear out my hair
> Cut off my limbs
> But leave me my love
>
> (Kane, 2001, 230)

Put differently, you can only love what you can lose. In his book, *The Noonday Demon: An Atlas of Depression*, Andrew Solomon (2014, 15) writes:

> Depression is the flaw in love. To be creatures who love, we must be creatures who can despair at what we lose, and depression is the mechanism of that despair. When it comes, it degrades one's self and ultimately eclipses the capacity to give or receive affection. It is the aloneness within us made manifest, and it destroys not only connection to others but also the ability to be peacefully alone with oneself.

We can see the resonances between Solomon's observation and the condition of Kane's 'I' that admonishes itself for a series of often contradictory physical and emotional deficiencies: 'I cannot be alone/ I cannot be with others/My hips are too big/I dislike my genitals' (207).

The trope of loss permeates *4.48 Psychosis*, but there is a perplexing ambiguity about who or what is lost. Alex Sierz provides us with a compelling insight into this mystery when he quotes Kane talking about her reading of Roland Barthes' *A Lover's Discourse*, which she used as an inspiration for her earlier play *Cleansed*:

> When I first read [Barthes's equation of a rejected lover and a prisoner in Dachau] I was appalled he could make the connection, but I couldn't stop thinking about it. And gradually I realized that Barthes is right: it is all about loss of self. When you love obsessively, you lose your sense of self. And if you lose the object of your love, you have no resources to fall back on. It can completely destroy you.
>
> (Kane quoted in Sierz 2000, 116)

William Styron believes that loss 'in all its manifestations is the touchstone of depression – in the progress of the disease and, most likely, in its origins' (1992, 56). In *4.48 Psychosis*, though, loss appears indivisibly linked to the experience of love.

In his book, *In Praise of Love*, Badiou argues that love is not for the faint-hearted, and the truth of love, one's fidelity to the event of love, 'is a unique trust placed in chance. It takes us into key areas of the experience of what is difference and, essentially, leads to the idea that you can experience the world from the perspective of difference' (2012, 16). Love, then,

literally reorients the way you look at the world, by demand-
ing the sacrifice of one's singular perspective; one becomes
two. However, love for Badiou cannot be 'conceived only as
an exchange of mutual favours or isn't calculated in advance
as a profitable investment, love really is a unique trust placed
in chance' (2012, 16).

This contingency, though, is also a source of anxiety,
especially if one's love for somebody remains unrequited –
for love cannot be bought or sold, it is something that must
be given freely for it to retain its integrity as love. Simon
Critchley puts it more eloquently when he observes (2015,
30–31):

> The logic of love is akin to the logic of grace. I give
> something that is truly beyond my capacity to control,
> I commit myself to it completely, but there can be no
> assurance that love will be reciprocated. At any point in
> a love relation, the beloved can and must be able to say
> 'I love you not'. If this is not the case, if the beloved can-
> not refuse love, then love is reduced to coercive control,
> contractual obligation and command.

While it is not clear whether the 'I' in *4.48 Psychosis* refers to
a single lover, or various lovers (including one of the doctors,
of which I shall say more in a moment), there is little doubt
that unrequited love plays a significant role in the work's pres-
entation of mental illness:

> Sometimes I turn around and catch the smell of you and
> I cannot go on I cannot fucking go on without express-
> ing this terrible so fucking awful physical aching fuck-
> ing longing I have for you. And I cannot believe that

I can feel this for you and you feel nothing. Do you feel nothing?

(*Silence.*)

Do you feel nothing?

(Kane, 2001, 214)

This passage captures the incredulity the speaker feels when she realises her lover does not reciprocate her intense feelings. This realisation is what is so frightening and exhilarating about love. You cannot compel another to love you, which means that to love is to live with the ever present possibility of loss. The 'I' in *4.48 Psychosis* experiences this prospect as debilitating anxiety.

Love is the drug: psychiatry, transference and depression

Let's keep our focus on the topic of love, but now in the context of psychiatry. *4.48 Psychosis* presents a scathing account of the way the medical profession treats people diagnosed with mental illness. The play makes several derisive references to the medical profession, especially in those fragments that suggest that the 'I' is kept under constant surveillance, and treated condescendingly (209):

I am deadlocked by that smooth psychiatric voice of reason which tells me there is an objective reality in which my body and mind are one. But I am not here and never have been. Dr This writes it down and Dr That attempts a sympathetic murmur. Watching me, judging me, smelling the crippling failure oozing from my skin, my desperation clawing and all-consuming panic drenching me

as I gape in horror at the world and wonder why everyone is smiling and looking at me with secret knowledge
of my aching shame.

I could cite several other passages that reinforce the view
that most medical professionals adopt an overly rational and
detached approach to the problem of mental illness. However,
I think it is sufficient to note, in the words of Singer, that
'to build scepticism about the psychiatric establishment, Kane
provides an extensive list of symptoms, diagnoses, and failed
medications' (2004, 34). The only glimmer of positivity in all
this takes the form of an empathetic doctor who treats the 'I' as
a singular human being rather than a defective mechanism by
'taking the piss', laughing at the patient's 'gallows humour' and
who lied 'and said it was nice to see [her/him/them]' (209).

The play suggests that the 'I' has perhaps fallen in love with
this distinctive figure: 'I loved you, and it's not losing you
that hurts me, but your bare-faced fucking falsehoods that
masquerade as medical notes' (210). It's possible to read this
relationship as dramatising the Freudian concept of transference, which accounts for the way doctors, analysts or other
authority figures such as teachers act as surrogates for people
in the patient's life. The patient transfers the feelings they have
for these familiar characters to the doctor, thereby reenacting
the dynamics of those possibly traumatic personal relation-
ships with the analyst (Freud, 1949). There is often an erotic
component to transference and Freud remarks that the analyst
needs to be vigilant while recognising the possible therapeu-
tic benefits of this phenomenon. He states (1949, 174) that a
patient may see the analyst as:

the reincarnation, of some important figure out of his
childhood or past, and consequently transfers on to him

feelings and reactions which undoubtedly applied to this prototype. This fact of transference soon proves to be a factor of undreamt-of importance, on the one hand an instrument of irreplaceable value and on the other hand a source of serious dangers.

Ariel Watson (2008) identifies the performative dimension of transference, and draws attention to the way the 'I' re-enacts the experience of loss and rejection with the play's empathetic doctor, who attempts to maintain a 'professional' distance while communicating on a human level:

—You don't need a friend you need a doctor.
(A long silence.)
—You are so wrong.
(A very long silence.)
—But you have friends.
(A long silence.)
You have a lot of friends.
What do you offer your friends to make them so supportive?…
We have a professional relationship. I think we have a good relationship.
But it's professional.
(Silence.)
I feel your pain but I cannot hold your life in my hands.
(Silence.)…
Most of my clients want to kill me. When I walk out of here at the end of the day
I need to go home to my lover and relax. I need to be with my friends and relax.
I need my friends to be really together.
(Silence.)

I fucking hate this job and I need my friends to be sane.
(Silence.)
I'm sorry.

(2001, 236–237)

After identifying with this empathetic figure because he
or she 'gets' the patient's gallows humour, and after stating that gestures of basic friendliness are more therapeuti-
cally valuable than medication, the 'I' re-enacts a form of
the rejection and loss that possibly led to its 'pathological
grief'. Kane, once again, invokes the tropes of love and loss,
thereby conveying the degree to which non-biological factors contribute to depression. Indeed, loss looms as such a
massive source of anguish that the 'I' even mourns the loss
of phantom lovers:

I dread the loss of her I've never touched
Love keeps me a slave in a cage of tears
I gnaw my tongue with which to her I can never speak
I miss a woman who was never born
I kiss a woman across the years that say we shall
    never meet

        Everything passes
        Everything perishes
        Everything palls

(2001, 218)

In short, the play consistently refers to what we might call
abandoned love. That said, we should be cautious about for-
mulating any single thesis about what may or may not precipitate mental illness, which manifests in various forms and

different degrees of intensity depending on the individual. After all, this is why it remains such a mysterious phenomenon. Singer points out that Kane carefully researched mental illness, and used her reading of medical texts concerned with the causes of mental illness in her play. She apparently read and utilised parts of Shneidman's *The Suicidal Mind* in *4.48 Psychosis* (Singer, 2004, 176). Of course, Kane's play draws on a variety of other intertextual sources, but it is worth focusing on the work's references to the medical literature on depression since the play is, as we have already seen, highly critical of the way the medical establishment approaches depression. The play's medical references make more sense if we situate Kane's critique of psychiatry within the context of social and medical history.

Diedrich argues that we must place Kane's withering assessment of the then orthodox approach to treating depression within the framework of the American Psychiatric Association's publication of the *Diagnostic and Statistical Manual of Mental Disorders (DSM-III)* in 1980, which transformed the diagnosis and treatment of mental illness (Diedrich, 2013, 378). In simple terms, this shift replaces the belief that repressed psychic impulses generate mental disorders with 'a biomedical model that categorised mental illnesses – like organic diseases – into discrete natural entities, clearly identifiable by clusters of symptoms' (Diedrich, 2013, 378). Moreover, this new biomedical conception of mental illness placed a greater emphasis on chemical imbalances in the brain as the leading cause of depressive maladies and advocated treating the disease with psychopharmacological drugs. Moreover, the new DSM regime established diagnostic criteria, which form the basis of the questionnaires doctors use to identify clinical depression. Kane

(2001, 223) invokes the diagnostic logic of the DSM in the following way:

SYMPTOMS: Not eating, not sleeping, not speaking, no sex drive, in despair, wants to die.
DIAGNOSIS: Pathological grief.

What follows is a harrowing catalogue of the speaker's frustration with pharmacological treatments, which culminates in a suicide attempt through the consumption of '100 aspirin and one bottle of Bulgarian Cabernet Sauvignon' (225). Singer points out that 'even with a list of a patient's symptoms and a list of drugs that work on him or her, we know neither what is malfunctioning nor why it is malfunctioning' (2004, 136).

However, the mystery at the heart of clinical depression is not the only issue at play in *4.48 Psychosis*. Watson argues that we also need to contextualise the play with reference to the British public's 'profound distrust of the National Health Service as well as a discomfort with both the Thatcherite deinstitutionalisation movement, known as 'care in the community', and the oppressive practices of the psychiatric hospitals themselves' (2008, 198). Kane makes direct reference to this form of 'care' when she writes about a doctor discharging a patient because of a lack of beds, and the hospitalisation of someone with an apparently more acute disorder (224). In simple terms, Kane was writing during a period marked by a scepticism towards conventional psychiatry and its use of pharmacological drugs, and the play resonates with the so-called 'anti-psychiatry' movement that argued that mental illness is primarily socially constructed (Watson, 2008). Ariel Watson identifies Michel Foucault, Erving Goffman, R. D. Laing and Thomas Szasz as the most prominent critics of psychiatry. In their own way, each of these writers identifies the ways medical institutions categorise people as sane or insane by using forms of rationality that preclude empathy. In short, they treat patients as objects of study and analysis rather than as human beings. In *The Divided Self*, Laing (1990, 21) writes:

> Now, if you are sitting opposite me, I can see you as another person like myself; without you changing or doing anything differently, I can now see you as a complex physical-chemical system, perhaps with its own idiosyncrasies but chemical none the less for that; seen in this way, you are no longer a person but an organism,

In short, Laing advocates engaging with so-called mentally ill people as *people*, first and foremost. This position resonates with those passages from *4.48 Psychosis*, cited above, which express frustration with the way hospitals de-humanise patients (2001, 209; 223–234).

Art and depression

In the final section of this chapter, I will briefly explain some of Michel Foucault's ideas about the relationship between madness and the work of artists deemed to be mad. Today, many people believe the word 'mad' unfairly stigmatises people suffering from depression. William Styron is not among those who hold this view. He wrote that 'our modern need to dull the sawtooth edges of so many of the afflictions we are heir to has led us to banish the harsh old-fashioned words: madhouse, asylum, insanity, melancholia, lunatic, madness. But never let it be doubted that depression in its extreme form is madness' (1992, 46–47). I understand there will be those who find the word 'mad' offensive, but I think it's worth suspending our sensitivities to engage with Foucault's argument, which provides valuable insights into the way we might reflect on the relationship between Kane's illness and her work.

In the final chapter of *Madness and Civilisation*, Foucault addresses the relationship between madness and art in the modern era by examining a handful of artists deemed to be mad. His remarks on the topic are opaque, yet germane to understanding the paradoxical status of Kane's play. As we observed with Singer in the last chapter, the critical reception of *4.48 Psychosis* takes two opposed positions. The first read the play in the light of her suicide while the second treated it as an intricate work of art irreducible to its author's mental illness. Foucault identifies an interesting paradox in the work of those artists deemed to be 'mad'. Put simply, he suggests that the artist's madness acts as a catalyst for the creation of the work of art, but also ultimately destroys the truth of the work (1964, 287). In other words, the ordeal of madness *coincides* with the void expressed within the work of art, but should not be mistaken for the work itself. This argument is difficult to grasp since Foucault asks us to acknowledge the centrality of the experience of madness to the creation of the work while imploring us to recognise that the madness of the artist obstructs the work's artistic qualities.

Foucault also points out that we celebrate and venerate artists deemed to be mad for the way they pose awkward questions about the relationship between reason and unreason. In other words, he believes that art produced by the likes of Artaud unsettles truths about the status of rationality itself.

Thus, Kane's play holds the world of reason to account by posing awkward questions about its treatment of those it considers mad. If we read *4.48 Psychosis* in the light of Foucault's arguments, we can better apprehend how we cannot disentangle the posthumous veneration of Kane's play from the horrors of her illness and its treatment by the medical profession. Having identified some of the critical connections between the work's representation of clinical depression, and the medical discourses on the diagnosis and treatment of this malady, we can now take a closer look at the play's formal properties with particular reference to the theory of postdramatic theatre before addressing how these elements work in performance.

References

Badiou, Alain (2012) *In Praise of Love*. Translated by Peter Bush. New York: The New Press.

Campbell, Alyson (2005) 'Experiencing Kane: an affective analysis of Sarah Kane's "experiential" theatre in performance'. *Australasian Drama Studies* 46: 80–97.

Camus, Albert (1979) *The Myth of Sisyphus*. Harmondsworth: Penguin.

Critchley, Simon (2015) *Suicide*. Williamsburg, NY: Thought Catalogue Books.

Diedrich, Antje (2013) '"Last in a Long Line of Literary Kleptomaniacs": Intertextuality in Sarah Kane's *4.48 Psychosis*'. *Modern Drama* 56:3: 374–398.

Esslin, Martin (2004) *The Theatre of the Absurd*. 3rd edition. New York: Random House.

Foucault, Michel (1964) *Madness and Civilisation: A History of Insanity in the Age of Reason*. Translated by Richard Howard. New York: Random House.

Freud, Sigmund (1949) *An Outline of Psycho-Analysis*. Translated by James Strachey. New York: W.W. Norton.

Freud, Sigmund (1957) 'Mourning and Melancholia'. Translated by James Strachey. *The Standard Edition of the Complete Psychological Works of Sigmund Freud, Volume XIV (1914–1916): On the History of the Psycho-Analytic Movement, Papers on Metapsychology and Other Works*. London: The Hogarth Press. Original publication, 1917.

Heidegger, Martin (1962) *Being and Time*. Translated by John Macquarie and Edward Robinson. Oxford: Blackwell.

Kane, Sarah (2001) *Complete Plays*. Ed. David Greig. London: Methuen.

Laing, R. D. (1990) *The Divided Self: An Existential Study in Sanity and Madness*. London: Penguin.

Sierz, Aleks (2001) *In-Yer-Face Theatre: British Drama Today*. London: Faber and Faber.

Singer, Annabelle (2004) 'Don't Want to Be This: the Elusive Sarah Kane'. *The Drama Review* XLVIII:2: 139–171.

Solomon, Andrew (2014) *The Noonday Demon: An Atlas of Depression*. New York: Scribner.

Styron, William (1992) *Darkness Visible: A Memoir of Madness*. New York: Random House.

Tycer, Alicia (2008) '"Victim, Perpetrator, Bystander": Melancholy Witnessing of Sarah Kane's *4.48 Psychosis*'. *Theatre Journal* 61:1: 23–36.

Watson, Ariel (2008) 'Cries of Fire: Psychotherapy in Contemporary British and Irish Drama'. *Modern Drama* 51:2: 188–210.

3

Theorising *4.48 Psychosis*

4.48 Psychosis as postdramatic theatre

What is postdramatic theatre? And why do critics and scholars regularly invoke this term in their analyses of *4.48 Psychosis*? Before addressing these questions directly, let's look closely at the play's form, and note how it departs from the conventions of realist theatre (that is, theatre concerned with representing clearly delineated dramatic characters in a fictional world). Despite its poetic qualities, there is no doubt that *4.48 Psychosis* is a text written for the theatre. The obvious giveaway is that the work appears in a book titled *Sarah Kane: Complete Plays* and its first page follows the convention of published dramatic texts by providing the details of the work's first performance. The first page of the play proper also underscores the performative dimension of the work by issuing an imperative in the form of a stage direction: '*(A very long silence.)*' (205). As the reader will soon discover, this, and Kane's use of the dash, a typographical figure I will return to, constitute the only real stage directions in the play. Most often, we find '*(Silence.)*' But these instructions are ambiguous. What precisely is '*(A long silence.)*' and how might it differ from '*(A really long silence.)*'? These are obviously not insignificant questions for those attempting to stage the play, for directors and performers need to pay close attention to how these imperatives work with the rhythm of the performance. On the page, it's difficult to evoke the effect of silence (unless you are reading aloud). The direction '*(A very long silence.)*' is also the first of many allusions or references to other texts. In this instance, it is impossible not to think of Harold Pinter, who turned silence into a powerful dramatic agent. Early in his career, Pinter made the following observation about the importance of silence in the theatre:

> You arrange and you listen, following the clues you leave for yourself, through the characters. And sometimes a balance is found, where image can freely engender image and where at the same time you are able to keep your sights on the place where the characters are silent and in hiding. It is in the silence that they are most evident to me.
>
> (Pinter quoted in Billington, 2009, 226)

Here, then, is our first clue about the place or status of *4.48 Psychosis* in the tradition of dramatic writing. Silence aside, the next thing we notice is that the first line of the text uses a dash in place of a proper name that designates the connection between the line and a distinct character. Kane was not the first dramatist to eschew this convention. German-language playwrights such as Peter Handke and Heiner Müller had also written works without designating conventional *dramatis personae*. Kane – as a graduate of a university drama course – may well have have been aware of these writers and would certainly have been aware of Martin Crimp's play *Attempts on Her Life*, which the Royal Court staged in 1997. This work also dispensed with many of the conventions we associate with dramatic writing – it presented seventeen scenarios for the theatre, which provided only the 'basic ingredients' for anyone wishing to stage the play. Each scene refers to a figure that goes by the name of Anne (and variants of Anne, such as Anya, Anna and so on) but Crimp provides no indication of specific locations or specific characters that are supposed to speak the lines of his play. Significantly for our present investigation, Crimp uses the humble dash to indicate the change of speaker, but otherwise provides scant information about how this work might be performed. Like Kane's play, *Attempts on Her Life* requires the creative team to make a set of creative decisions about staging the work without the conventional prompts written into most plays. The question of who speaks, and whom the first line of *4.48 Psychosis* might address is ambiguous. We might hazard a guess, and assume that a single person is addressing someone who remains mute and is presumably a figure suffering from psychosis. The dash indicates a single speaker, but there's no reason why a director need follow this direction in performance. This first section of the play is separated from the next by centrally placed dashes. The following part of the text is even more confounding:

> a consolidated consciousness resides in a darkened banqueting hall near the ceiling of a mind whose floor shifts as ten thousand cockroaches when a shaft of light enters as all thoughts unite in an instant of accord body no longer expellent as the cockroaches comprise a truth which no one ever utters

> I had a night in which everything was revealed to me. How can I speak again?

the broken hermaphrodite who trusted hermself alone
finds the room in reality teeming and begs never to wake
from the nightmare

> and they were all there
> every last one of them
> and they knew my name
> as I scuttled like a beetle along the backs of their
>   chairs

Remember the light and believe the light

An Instant of Clarity before eternal night

(2001, 205–206)

This does not look like conventional dramatic writing, yet if
we examine the text closely, we can see that it functions as a
form of exposition that introduces several of the play's key
themes and motifs. Let's pause and unpack this observation.
The typography of the first part of this second section ignores
grammatical conventions by eschewing punctuation marks
that usually indicate how we might perform a dramatic text.
The next couple of indented lines do use conventional punctuation, and this contrast between apparently unstructured
poetic language and moments of lucidity is a feature of the
play. The play – as many critics have pointed out – resembles
a modernist poem in the way Kane presents it on the page.
The poetic quality of the language is most evident in the first
part of the extract above. As I read it, the passage presents a
striking, dream-like image of a 'consolidated consciousness'
(a subject, an 'I') trapped in a space overrun by 'thousands of
cockroaches'. This frightening metaphor of madness gives way
to some lines of clarity before the poetic register resumes with

a reference to 'the broken hermaphrodite' trapped in a nightmare world. Kane coins the pronoun 'hermself' to refer to this personage, and in doing so introduces the theme of sexual identity, or – more properly – the theme of sexual ambiguity that may be a component of the anguish experienced by the 'I', the sometime consolidated consciousness. The passage also resonates with Kafka's famous novella *The Metamorphosis*, which tells the story of a man who transforms into a beetle. This absurd tale depicts the protagonist's struggle to adjust to his newfound state of being, and his gradual alienation from his family and everyday life. This theme of alienation, prefigured here in the first part of the play, functions as a motif that gives the play an almost musical structure through its distribution throughout the text – it's a bit like a recurrent melodic phrase in a sonata, or a chorus in a pop song.

The play's final reference to the 'light' and the opposition that is set up between the clarity of the light and the darkness of the banqueting hall is another important structural feature of the play. In short, the repetition of these motifs gives the play a robust form. As we read on, we find a set of other unusual stylistic features. Some sections of the work consist of numbers (208; 232). Tycer provides a concise summary of the play's formal characteristics:

> The page layout varies throughout the play, ranging from dialogue, to lists, columns, and a few numbers or words scattered on a page. Scenes are delineated by a series of dashes instead of the traditional act and scene divisions, with the urgent acronym 'RSVP ASAP' (214) being the shortest example of a scene. Kane calls attention to word choice, even of seemingly insignificant words: 'No ifs or buts. / I didn't say if or but, I said no' (219).
>
> (Tycer, 2008, 26–27)

Scholars in theatre and performance studies have made the term 'postdramatic' an integral part of their critical vocabulary since Hans-Thies Lehmann published the English translation of his book, *Postdramatic Theatre* in 2006 (he wrote the original German edition in 1999). Critics regularly invoke the term when referring to *4.48 Psychosis* (Lehmann, 2006; Barnett, 2008; D'Cruz, 2010; Delgado-García, 2012; Roberts, 2015). So, let's return to the question I posed at the start of this chapter: what is postdramatic theatre, and how does the concept resonate with Kane's play? Unfortunately, there is no simple answer to this question. As Marvin Carlson points out – 'anything like a coherent and consistent definition of the term has become quite impossible', and 'there is no theatrical phenomenon to which it refers that cannot be traced back in theatre practice to times long before the term began to be applied' (2015).

For our purposes though, the concept is perhaps best understood as something that refers to work concerned with liberating performance from the realist conventions of dramatic literature. That is, from the idea that drama should represent a self-contained fictional world in which characters tell a story by spouting dialogue to create dramatic tension in the pursuit of specific objectives. Lehmann believes that plays that merely tell stories about the trials and tribulations of characters that are supposed to represent real people can no longer convey complex ideas about present-day society. He proposes that the most significant works of contemporary theatre over the last 50 years or so haven't been dependent on texts written by playwrights. Whereas the composed 'play' was once the thing that functioned as the primary source for a theatrical performance, many contemporary artists see the dramatic text as a single component among a melange of theatrical tools.

It is important to stress that the term 'postdramatic' does not strictly refer to works produced within a particular period or geographical location. Rather it relates to a *rupture* that signals a *drift* between the dramatic text and theatrical performance, so the play script is not necessarily the starting point for theatrical performance. Moreover, this separation between text and performance undermines the authority of both the dramatic text and the author as the creator of the work. Critics regularly categorise as 'postdramatic' a broad range of works that precede Lehmann's formulation of the term. The work of New York's experimental theatre company, the Wooster Group serves as a useful example of the way postdramatic theatre reconfigures the relationship between text and performance. Writing in 1985, Arnold Aronson points out (65) that the Wooster Group

> has taken modern classics (*The Cocktail Party*, *Long Day's Journey into Night*, *Our Town* and *The Crucible*) as raw material upon which to construct theatre pieces. Out of these sources come fragments of scenes, characters, dialog and thematic material which are explored, reworked, echoed, quoted, blended and juxtaposed with fragments from popular, cultural and social history as well as events, ideas and situations that emerge from the personal and collective experiences of members of the group.

The Wooster Group are not concerned with conveying authorial intentions or respecting the integrity of the dramatic text. Rather, they are more interested in using the text as a point of departure for their creative agenda. Moreover, if a written text is a component of a postdramatic performance, it carries no more authority than any other element of the performance – such as the way a director organises bodies in space or uses props, lighting, music and other sound effects to convey a particular atmosphere or set of affects. Lehmann (2006, 85) argues that the word 'postdramatic':

> best describes those contemporary performance works that employ 'new' forms of sign usage that privilege presence over representation, process over product and unsettle the status of hermetically sealed fictional worlds situated in a specific time and place.

In other words, postdramatic theatre does not seek to represent a distinct, recognisable world, nor does it attempt to tell a linear story that follows the realist conventions outlined above. Let's break down this statement by comparing *4.48 Psychosis* with Kane's first play, *Blasted* (1995), while recalling Kane's declaration that she found performance more interesting than literary drama.

Despite its notoriety, *Blasted* is, in many ways, a conventional play, at least until Kane blows up the fictional world she creates in the first part of the work. If we look at the first few pages of the published text, we can see that Kane identifies three distinct characters: Ian, Cate and Soldier. She gives Ian and Cate specific biographical attributes: 'Ian is 45, Welsh born but lived in Leeds much of his life and picked up the accent' (3). She provides details of the play's setting: '*A very expensive hotel room in Leeds – the kind that is so expensive it could be anywhere in the world*' (3). She specifies other details about this location, divides the play into clearly marked scenes, and assigns dialogue to each of the three characters. This is not to say the play is wholly naturalistic. As previously noted, the second half of the play shatters the fictional world set up in the first part of the work but continues to unfold according to a dramatic logic determined by standard notions of character and dialogue. Today, *Blasted* is remembered for its sexual violence and gore – the soldier rapes Ian, shoves a rifle up his arse before shooting him and sucking out one of his eyeballs. This is obviously not a scene that resonates with the work of Ibsen (or Pinter, for that matter). It is, however, most definitely 'In-Yer-Face'. My point is that *Blasted* is – on the page at least – easily recognisable as a play. The form of *4.48 Psychosis* is something else. As previously stated, instead of characters, scenes and demarcated dialogue we have 'bewildered fragments' (2001, 210). The question I want to probe in the final section of this chapter is whether the concept of postdramatic theatre contributes anything useful to our understanding of *4.48 Psychosis*.

Beyond its apparent rejection of dramatic conventions on the page, how might we understand the relationship between *4.48 Psychosis* and postdramatic theatre? David Barnett suggests that Kane's play is postdramatic insofar as it eschews representation, temporal linearity, and flaunts its references to other works (some of which I identified in the previous chapter). On the topic of representation, Barnett argues that 'there are poetic meditations on depression that organize themselves on the page in ways that simply cannot be represented in an unambiguous fashion on stage' (2008, 21). Indeed, it is this ambiguity that makes the play such a malleable entity – it requires the director to decide how to locate these 'meditations' in the theatre space without the customary stage directions. Furthermore, the play 'does not offer a linear time structure' (2008, 21). In other words, don't go looking for a traditional beginning, middle or end in *4.48 Psychosis*. However, this is not to say the play lacks a temporal structure.

As I've already indicated Kane repeats motifs and language throughout the work. The most obvious example of this is the repetition of the phrase 'At 4.48' (207; 213; 229; 233). This titular line refers to the time when 'depression visits' and after a time when the 'I' 'won't speak again' (207; 213). It is also the time 'when sanity visits' and, finally, the time 'when I shall lie asleep'. Barnett points out that Kane 'has certainly arranged and ordered her scenes – there are repetitions, echoes, and changes in cadence – but there is neither cause, nor effect, nor development. The condition is not explained, no answers are proffered' (2008, 21–22). Perhaps Barnett's most astute insight occurs when he observes that:

> although one could interpret the speeches, humanize them, and represent characters and conversations, the text itself offers a very different potential in performance: the chance to turn a human theatre into a theatre of language, where the performers are responsible for the imaginative presentation of linguistic material which is then experienced and processed by the audience.

Barnett's phrase 'a theatre of language' refers to the possibility of articulating the lines without regard for their literal meanings, but for their rhythmic and sonic possibilities. In her article about Philip Venables' operatic adaptation of the play, Cristina Delgado-García observes that 'the text of *4.48 Psychosis* invites us not to understand the external reality of its speakers, but to feel the pulse of images, timbres, rhythms, patterns. It requires that we grasp emotions through cadences, often beyond the meaning of words' (2016). One of the central tenets of Lehmann's concept of the 'postdramatic' concerns the necessity of finding new theatrical languages to convey the experience of living in a world where 'a simul-taneous and multi-perspectival form of perceiving is replac-ing the linear-successive' (2006, 16). Lehmann is referring to the way new media technologies saturate everyday life and bombard us with a constant flow of images and sound bites that alter the way we process information. Our 'society of the spectacle' – to use Guy Debord's term (1995) – also blurs the distinction between the real and virtual, the original and the copy in unprecedented ways.

However, Kane's dream-like images have more to do with psychotic perception than the society of the spectacle. While she does not refer to Kane's play in her paper 'Did you mean post-traumatic theatre?', Karen Jürs-Munby provides another useful way to read *4.48 Psychosis* under the rubric of post-dramatic theatre when she asks whether there might be similarities between the experience of trauma – which resists conventional narrative modes of representation – and post-dramatic theatre's tendency to avoid traditional story telling (2009, 1). She cites Cathy Caruth's observation that post-trau-matic experience often 'takes the forms of repeated, intrusive hallucinations, dreams, thoughts or behaviors stemming from this event, along with numbing that may have begun during or after the experience, and possibly also increased arousal to (and avoidance of) stimuli recalling the event' (1996, 4). If we accept this thesis, it's evident that Kane structured her play by following a post-traumatic logic.

On the other hand, some people challenge the view that *4.48 Psychosis* dispenses with traditional dramatic conceptions of drama. For example, Delgado-García makes a convincing case that the concept of character still provides a useful way into understanding Kane's work. She claims that the idea of character 'is any figuration of subjectivity, any theatrical outline of human existence, regardless of how individuated or, conversely, how unmarked its contours might be' (2012, 231). This argument also draws on Judith Butler's idea that human subjectivity is relational, and that the loss of a close lover, relative or friend can shatter your sense of identity (2004). In other words, if the beloved other is part of what makes the individual unique, the loss of the beloved throws the subject into crisis – the person becomes 'inscrutable' to itself (2004, 22). Delgado-García's point, then, is that while the play does not represent the standard liberal-humanist subject – that is, a common-sense understanding of the individual as an autonomous human being with agency – it does not wholly dispense with the concept of character. Rather, it presents a different, traumatic mode of subjectivity.

Before leaving the topic of the play's relationship to post-dramatic theory, it is worth mentioning that one of the dangers in writing a work that requires a greater degree of input from directors and actors is that some readers and critics may undervalue the work's status as writing, or contest its quality as writing. I firmly believe Kane's play is well written and carefully structured. However, there are dissenting opinions about the quality of Kane's written text. Mary Luckhurst, for example, declares that 'I am not of the view that Kane was a great writer nor that her plays represented a defining moment' (2002, 72). Indeed, she attributes much of Kane's early success to the theatrical imagination and resourcefulness of James Macdonald, whose productions of Kane's work – in Luckhurst's opinion – 'outclasses the writing' (2002, 72). Even Aleks Sierz, one of Kane's earliest champions, acknowledges Kane's limitations as a writer. He points out that she was not good at writing naturalistic dialogue, for example. However, her writing shines when, as Sierz infers, she is creating or suggesting a stage image or advancing an argument (Sierz quoted in Saunders, 2009, 124). As we shall see in Chapter 5, directors and performers have found plenty of imaginative ways to stage *4.48 Psychosis*, but I think there are good reasons for why they are drawn to this play. I believe it is churlish to dismiss Kane's writing as a significant factor in the success of *4.48 Psychosis*. Granted, you need a theatrical imagination to appreciate the play on the page. Reading this work is not like reading *A Streetcar Named Desire*, or *Angels in America*. If you are looking for well-drawn characters speaking naturalistic dialogue, you need to look elsewhere. Kane is simply not that kind of writer, but in my view, she articulated a singular vision about what it's like to suffer from crippling depression in *4.48 Psychosis*, and this is an achievement worth acknowledging and celebrating. Perhaps her celebrity and her posthumous status as an icon, 'Saint Sarah' the doomed youth, function as the greatest impediments to appreciating her talent as a writer. I hope my explication of the themes and structure of *4.48 Psychosis* demonstrate its value as dramatic writing. The following chapters will focus on the play in performance from the perspective of teachers and practitioners and will reinforce the view that Kane was a talented playwright.

References

Aronson, Arnold (1985) 'The Wooster Group's L.S.D. (…just the high points…)'. *The Drama Review* 29:2: 64–77.

Barnett, David (2008) 'When is a Play not a Drama? Two Examples of Postdramatic Theatre Texts'. *New Theatre Quarterly* 24:1:14–23.

Billington, Michael (2009) *Harold Pinter*. London: Faber and Faber.

Butler, Judith (2004) *Precarious Life: The Powers of Mourning and Violence*. London and New York: Verso.

Carlson, Marvin (2015) 'Postdramatic Theatre and Postdramatic Performance'. *Brazilian Journal of Presence Studies* 5:3: http://dx.doi.org/10.1590/2237-266053731.Accessed 24 April 2017.

Caruth, Cathy (1996) *Unclaimed Experience: Trauma, Narrative, and History*. Baltimore, MD: Johns Hopkins University Press.

Crimp, Martin (1997) *Attempts on Her Life*. London and Boston, MA: Faber and Faber.

D'Cruz, Glenn (2010) 'Teaching/Directing *4.48 Psychosis*'. *Australasian Drama Studies* 57: 99–114.

Debord, Guy (1995) *The Society of the Spectacle*. Translated by Donald Nicholson-Smith. New York: Zone Books. Original publication 1967.

Delgado-García, Cristina (2016) 'Why Sarah Kane's Play *4.48 Psychosis* is the Perfect Inspiration for an Opera', The Royal Opera House www.roh.org.uk/news/why-sarah-kanes-play-4-48-psychosis-is-the-perfect-candidate-for-an-operatic-adaptation. Accessed 27 July 2017.

Delgado-García, Cristina (2012) 'Subversion, Refusal, and Contingency: The Transgression of Liberal-Humanist Subjectivity and Characterization in Sarah Kane's *Cleansed*, *Crave*, and *4.48 Psychosis*'. *Modern Drama* 55:2: 230–250.

Foucault, Michel (1964) *Madness and Civilisation: A History of Insanity in the Age of Reason*. Translated by Richard Howard. New York: Random House.

Jürs-Munby, Karen (2009) '"Did you Mean Post-Traumatic Theatre?": The Vicissitudes of Traumatic Memory in Contemporary Postdramatic Performances'. *Performance Paradigm* 5:2 www.performanceparadigm.net/wp-content/uploads/2009/10/jurs-munby-posttraumatic-postdramatic-final-copy-with-images.pdf. Accessed 27 July 2017.

Kafka, Franz (2007) *Metamorphosis and Other Stories*. Translated by Michael Hoffman. London: Penguin. Original publication, 1915.

Kane, Sarah (2001) *Complete Plays*. Ed. David Greig. London: Methuen.

Lehmann, Hans-Thies (2006) *Postdramatic Theatre*. Translated and with an afterword by Karen Jürs-Munby. London and New York: Routledge.

Luckhurst, Mary (2002) 'An Embarrassment of Riches: Women Dramatists in 1990s Britain', in Bernhard Reitz and Mark Berninger (eds), *British Drama of the 1990s*. Anglistik und Englischunterricht 64 (Heidelberg: Winter).

Roberts, Matthew (2015) 'Vanishing Acts: Sarah Kane's Texts for Performance and Postdramatic Theatre'. *Modern Drama* 58:1: 94–111.

Saunders, Graham (2009) *About Kane: the Playwright and the Work*. London: Faber and Faber.

Solomon, Andrew (2014) *The Noonday Demon: An Atlas of Depression*. New York: Scribner.

Tycer, Alicia (2008) 'Victim, Perpetrator, Bystander': Melancholy Witnessing of Sarah Kane's *4.48 Psychosis*'. *Theatre Journal* 61:1: 23–36.

4

Teaching *4.48 Psychosis*

Performance and pedagogy

4.48 Psychosis is a hugely popular play, if only measured by the number of search engine hits generated by typing its title into Google. The last time I did this, Google found 113,000 references to the work. If you head over to YouTube, you'll find a staggering number of videos related to *4.48 Psychosis* (11,200 and counting as of November 2017). A significant number of these videos present extracts from student productions of the play. Love it or loathe it, it's impossible to ignore the fact that Kane's last play – which may be her most enduring legacy – is a hit with various educational institutions. Indeed, YouTube provides a fascinating archive of the play in performance and reveals a remarkably diverse range of approaches to staging the text.

Now it's one thing to teach Sarah Kane's plays as dramatic literature, but quite another to stage them within a pedagogical context. *Blasted*, for example, presents an obvious set of problems – not least of all, finding a way to stage scenes depicting fellatio, frottage, rape, defecation and cannibalism with a student cast. *Phaedra's Love* and *Cleansed* throw up similar problems for those teachers taking a practice-based approach to teaching Kane's work. *Crave* and *4.48 Psychosis* are much easier prospects since they lack the overt representations of sexual violence and cruelty, but even these plays are not without their problems. In this chapter, I will identify some of the ethical and practical problems generated by staging this play with university students. I'm obviously one of many people who have directed this play within an academic context, where it seems to have found a niche as part of the contemporary drama curriculum (in a surprisingly wide range of geographical locations). Before engaging with the details of the production I directed at Deakin University in 2007, I will provide a general account of some of the possible difficulties the play poses for the pedagogue.

I had been teaching *4.48 Psychosis* as a workshop text for two or three years before deciding to stage it in its entirety in 2007, within the context of a production unit called ACP280: Performance, Text, Realisation. The following learning objectives appeared in the university handbook:

Topics to be addressed in this unit include:

- the nature of dramatic language,
- structure and theatrical style,
- the ways in which these work together to create dramatic meaning.

(Deakin University, 2007, 230)

The course aims to teach students something about the process of how to approach a dramatic text from the perspective of a practitioner. The rationale of the course, then, requires students to solve a series of practical staging problems. As previously mentioned, the postdramatic qualities of Kane's play – its lack of plot, detailed stage directions and *dramatis personae* – make it especially flexible in terms of practical staging options. My class comprised of 25 students, and I was determined to give each member of the group an equal opportunity to contribute to the production not only as a performer but also as a deviser. After all, staging the play with a large group requires a considerable amount of creative input from everyone involved in the work. How do we allocate lines? How might we determine the location for each segment of the play? These challenges spoke directly to the learning objectives of the unit. However, I must confess that while I walked into the room with a few ideas about how to approach the work, I paid scant regard to the issue of how the students might respond to the play's harrowing themes.

Figure 4.1 Deakin University student production of *4.48 Psychosis*. Photograph: Glenn D'Cruz.

Teaching the play within the context of a workshop course about contemporary drama posed a few problems. Firstly, while I explicated the play through lectures and group discussions with the entire cohort of students, nobody was compelled to stage an extract from the work unless they decided to do so voluntarily. At Deakin University we do not audition students for productions that are part of our core curriculum. As a lecturer, I am required to stage and devise plays with whoever walks through the door of our rehearsal spaces. Our students come from a variety of ethnic, religious and socio-economic backgrounds, and it is impossible to know what sort of experiences – traumatic or otherwise – they bring with them. Today, I am much more conscious of the ethical problems posed by staging a play like *4.48 Psychosis* than I was ten years ago. This is because I now work within an institutional context that is risk averse, and, quite rightly, concerned with maintaining the duty of care that all teachers have towards their students. The institution now requires us to carry out risk assessments for any activity that might result in physical or psychological injury. This means that we need to be mindful of the fact that a play such as *4.48 Psychosis* may function as a 'trigger' for those students who struggle with depression or other forms of mental illness. Moreover, if we stage a play for the public, we are now also required to issue clear 'trigger warnings' to preclude the possibility of audience members being disturbed by confronting language, images and actions. I don't recall whether I was compelled to issue any 'trigger warnings' back in 2007, but I'm sure I would have to take a more cautious approach to staging the play today.

As it happened, none of the 25 students in the group objected to the play's content, although, as we shall see, not all of them expressed enthusiasm for the project. What might have happened had one or more of the students objected to my choice of text? And what might the consequences have been if a student had felt traumatised by the process of staging the play? As it turned out, I did not have to respond to these questions. However, I did not have to solve other problems.

Rehearsals: several types of ambiguity

I always feel a sense of excitement and trepidation as I clear my throat and announce that it's time to make a start, even though I know that I will experience myriad problems and frustrations before opening night. Of course, my process begins with a close reading of the play. Like most teachers and directors, I have a game plan. I never walk into a rehearsal without having done a significant amount of preparation. However, this doesn't mean that I research the life of the playwright in exhaustive detail, or immerse myself in theoretical debates about what constitutes a postdramatic play.

First and foremost, I focus on the words on the page. I read the play from beginning to end, and make notes about those aspects of the text that interest me – figures of speech, images, metaphors, intertextual references. I'm looking for a point of departure, something that will allow me to bring something new and distinctive to the realisation of the play in performance. More often than not, I'm looking for something that will make my students connect with the work, and hold the attention of an audience who mostly comprise other drama students as well as friends and family of the cast. I might find a phrase or a thematic motif that initiates a chain of associations, which suggest a way to begin the performance. I want to make the postdramatic text intelligible and entertaining without compromising its formal characteristics.

As it turned out, the first few lines of *4.48 Psychosis* gave me the key to the play after I read a newspaper story about a teenage suicide pact on the internet. The story was the 'association' that I was looking for as a point of departure for my production. Here is an extract from the report:

> The two girls were part of a subculture known as emo, named after a type of music characterised by emotion and a confessional tone. Emo fans are stereotypically intro-verted, sensitive, moody and alienated, and are derided by other subcultures for self-pitying poetry commonly posted on MySpace.
>
> (Oaks, 2007)

The story was headline news all over Australia and gener-ated a media frenzy and moral panic about the dangers of the internet. As the parent of a teenager, I was aware of how important social networking internet sites like MySpace are to adolescents (MySpace was the dominant form of social media in 2007). I was also mindful of the fact that MySpace was a site where 'friends' communicated and interacted. Kane's play begins by referring to friends:

> (A very long silence)
> – But you have friends.
> (A long silence)
> You have lots of friends.
> What do you offer your friends to make them so supportive?
>
> (Kane, 2001, 205)

Linking MySpace friends and the friends in Kane's text provided me with a concrete image for the play's beginning.
I walked into the rehearsal knowing two things. The first was
that the production would begin with two characters sitting
on chairs in the middle of the space, their faces illuminated
by the glow of laptop computer screens and the spill from
a projection from a fake MySpace site. The second was that
this image risked sensationalising suicide and detracting from
the admirable restraint evident in Kane's elegant writing.
Moreover, I was mindful of the fact that making such an overt
reference to the recent tragedy could be construed as insensi-
tive and even exploitative.

Nonetheless, I decided to go ahead with the 'emo' inter-
pretation of *4.48 Psychosis* – not because I thought that it
was a powerful artistic strategy, but because I believed that
it would provide my students with a series of pedagogically
instructive aesthetic and ethical dilemmas. I was aware that
most people on MySpace also used instant messaging ser-
vices like MSN to communicate with their friends online.
I decided that we would superimpose the first few lines of
Kane's text as an MSN instant message over the top of a pro-
jected MySpace profile on a large screen behind the two girls
with laptops. I usually have a predefined strategy for staging
the first scene of a production, but I find that the quality
of the work improves dramatically when the students feel as
though they can make a substantial creative contribution to
the play. But before inviting them to come up with their own
ways of realising the text in performance, I introduce the play
then ask each student to answer a few questions.

In the case of *4.48 Psychosis*, I asked them what they
could tell me about 'emo' subculture, and what they knew
about postdramatic theatre. Predictably, most could answer

the first question with confidence and authority, while they all struggled to provide coherent definitions of the postdramatic – even though they had all been introduced to the term in another course during the previous semester. As it turned out, the responses to my questions didn't tell me much that I didn't already know. This is not always the case. When I directed *Hamletmachine* in the same unit during the previous year, I asked each student to tell me what they knew about the Cold War. Their answers, with one or two exceptions, revealed an astounding ignorance of recent European history – or at least what I considered to be recent history. Why should I expect the average twenty-year-old to know anything about the fall of communism? The responses to the question about the Cold War made me wonder if ignorance about this period of history was more widespread, and provided me with a concrete starting point for the production. The one-on-one question and answer session is an important part of my process, even when the responses do not yield any useful information or insight into the play. It's important to find out how much the students already know about the themes of the work they are about to engage with, and it is also important for me to establish some rapport with each student at the project's outset. Students are often a little nervous, and even intimidated by this practice, but I persist with it because it helps me to get a sense of the students' personalities.

This is the process I followed. Having got a sense of who was in the class, and what they knew about 'emo' culture and postdramatic theatre, I distributed copies of the play to each student. We read the play as a group, and I asked them to share their immediate impressions of the work with their peers. Their responses didn't differ from the scholarly descriptions of the work's formal properties identified in earlier chapters of this book. I collated the students' comments on a white board: they discovered that on the page, *4.48 Psychosis* looked like a series of poems mostly written in blank verse and comprised of lists and slabs of prose separated into discrete sections by a series of dashes. Some parts resembled traditional dramatic writing insofar as they suggested dramatic interaction between characters, even though Kane didn't introduce any 'characters' as such. Others are – at first glance anyway – random arrangements of numbers. There is no uniformity in the length of each section – some are incredibly short, with one consisting of nothing more than the acronyms 'RSVP ASAP'. Some of the students were horrified by the prospect of staging the play and were not shy in voicing their concerns about putting on a play that doesn't tell a story or present recognisable characters that are sympathetic and exciting. One asked why I wanted to stage something that is so depressing. I explained that Kane's play, as I read it, is remarkably moving, and provides a rare insight into an issue that many people would rather ignore. I added that, like most good drama, Kane's work gives us an opportunity to engage with a disturbing aspect of life with a degree of critical distance (or words to that effect). The student looked unconvinced, and I felt slightly embarrassed by the glibness of my response. Thankfully, most of the 25 people in the room were engaged and appeared ready to work.

The Q&A session, the read-through and the subsequent discussion took about two hours of the first class. In the remaining time, I divided the class into small groups and gave them extracts from the play and asked them to present a performed reading. Most struggled with the exercise and immediately took a comedic approach to the play. The work is not without moments of black humour, but I made it clear that I wanted to avoid 'sketch comedy'. The exercise yielded a couple of compelling performances, which I incorporated into the production. One group read out the numbers that appear on page 208 of the text as though they were bingo numbers. I liked the association of depression with a game of chance, since the manifestation of depression – when not induced by environmental factors or specific traumatic events in a person's life – is a matter of chance, a matter of inheriting specific genes that are continually shuffled as they move from one generation to the next. Another group, some of whom are dancers, interpreted the 'flash, flicker, slash, burn' section as choreographed movement using Laban's classification of human movement as their inspiration. I was heartened that the students treated the text as a starting point for a performance, as opposed to a sacred piece of writing that demands fidelity to authorial intention. At the end of the session, I asked them to come to the next class with a prepared performance that showcased any hidden talents they may possess. If they could sing, dance, play a musical instrument or blow smoke out of their ears, I wanted to know about it.

This 'party trick' class gave me the opportunity to see the students perform for each other in a supportive environment. I find this exercise, more often than not, generates a bond between members of the cast that acts as a social emollient. However, the group turned out to be extremely fractious, and the rehearsal process exposed the various levels of inter-est and commitment to the project. The mini-performances revealed that some students were talented musicians; oth-ers were enthusiastic, though far from accomplished, musi-cians; others could dance; one student had sophisticated graphic design skills; another happened to be an expert in the

intricacies of MySpace aesthetics. I videotaped the performances and reviewed the tape to see how I might be able to
use the students' hidden talents productively, and I decided to
incorporate three short video segments into the production.
I asked the film students in my group to shoot three short
sequences that alluded to a recent newspaper story about
teenage suicides in an outer suburb of Melbourne. They duly
complied and come back a few weeks later with tasteful, non-
sensational images of a train journey into the hills, and shots
of a girl walking through the bush land and finally fading into
the air. The students did not attempt to dramatise or represent
the suicides.

I also utilised the skills of the musicians and dancers in the
ensemble. I had enough competent musicians to form a band
and provide live musical accompaniment to some sections of
the play. At the risk of stating the obvious, music is a highly
efficient mechanism for setting the tone of a performance,
and I wanted to establish what I will call – for want of a better
term – a melancholic atmosphere that matched the tenor of
Kane's writing. I asked the 'band' to learn Nick Drake's song
'Way to Blue', which I find haunting and atmospheric, and
then asked them to segue into 'Love Will Tear Us Apart' – a
song by Sarah Kane's favourite band, Joy Division, which had
recently been covered with a cheesy bossa nova feel by the
French group Nouvelle Vague, the version we used. I also got
the musicians to improvise sounds to add texture to various
sections of the play.

The development of these musical and multimedia elements helped to give the students a sense of ownership over
the production, and, once again, underscored its postdramatic aesthetic. Since the production is part of a course that
aims to provide students with the skills to generate their own

creative work, there seemed little point in my attempting to micro-manage the production. Having established a general concept and emotional tenor for the production, I divided them into groups and assigned them sections of the play to interpret and perform. I monitored their progress closely and made suggestions for amending sections that didn't work in practice. More often than not, I felt more like a project manager than a theatre director. However, giving students license to exercise their creativity is crucial to my process. On the few occasions when I had to scrap entire scenes, they responded with a remarkable degree of maturity. A dictatorial approach to direction, I suspect, is far more likely to breed resentment and indifference towards the artistic outcome of the process.

One especially problematic scene was the section where Kane's writing adopts a biblical tone and rhythm (228):

> We are anathema
> The pariahs of reason
> Why am I stricken?
> I saw visions of God
> And it shall come to pass

The students were having difficulty with Kane's shift in register until I suggested that we play the scene as though the speakers were evangelical preachers addressing a frenzied crowd of religious zealots. The night before this particular rehearsal, I had watched a documentary on Jim Jones, the American preacher infamously responsible for the Jonestown Massacre in 1978. This prompted me to appropriate the tone and rhythms of Jones' style of preaching. The cast gladly took this direction and energised the scene.

This is not to say that the process of mounting the play was without its challenges. Apart from the practical staging problems generated by the script, the process of directing the play with students required me to manage student absences from rehearsals and varying levels of commitment to the project (not everyone was equally committed to the production, and a small coterie of five or so students put minimal effort into rehearsals). In fact, the class was perhaps the most peevish and volatile that I have ever taught. Nonetheless, some of the postdramatic qualities of Kane's play (its lack of distinct characters with allocated lines) made it ideally suited to being performed by a large student cast. Most traditional dramatic plays only have a few principal roles, which means having to represent single characters with multiple actors or having the majority of the cast relegated to carrying spears and intoning choral speeches. In short, the play is well suited to educational contexts. The fact that the students, under my guidance, had to make important creative decisions about how to stage the play enabled me, hopefully, to provide them with an opportunity to learn about dramatic structure and language, and give them the chance to solve practical staging problems.

As we have seen, directing the play within an educational context generates a unique set of challenges. Teachers have a duty of care towards students that preclude certain staging options (nudity is not an option, for example); there are also institutional regulations concerned with assessment and learning objectives that shape and delimit how students might perform the play. In the final chapter of the book, we will examine the way two professional theatre companies staged *4.48 Psychosis* to explore further how staging the play enables a greater appreciation of its aesthetic and political value.

References

Deakin University (2007) *Deakin University Undergraduate Handbook*. Melbourne: Deakin University.

Kane, Sarah (2001) *Complete Plays*. Ed. David Greig London: Methuen.

Oaks, Dan (2007) 'MySpace clues to teen death pact'. *The Sydney Morning Herald* www.smh.com.au/news/technology/myspace-clues-to-teen-death-pact/2007/04/23/1177180493150.html. Accessed 27 July 2017.

5

Performing 4.48 Psychosis

From Minsk to Melbourne

Sarah Kane did not live to see *4.48 Psychosis* performed on stage. She hanged herself on 20 February 1999, and the play premiered on 23 June 2000 at the Royal Court Theatre Upstairs in London. Since then it has been translated into several languages and performed all over the world. As I have argued throughout this book, the play's unorthodox form encourages directors, designers and actors to take an experimental approach to staging the work, so I will begin this chapter by briefly noting some of the play's most famous productions before dealing with two in detail. But let's first recall the inaugural performance of the play directed by James Macdonald with a cast of three actors: Daniel Evans, Jo McInnes and Madeleine Porter. A little before the premiere of Philip Venables' award-winning opera version of *4.48 Psychosis*, Macdonald and his actors reminisced about the play's first production with journalist Andrew Dixon. Dixon's story reveals that all three performers memorised the entire text, so the articulation of particular speeches depended on who got the impulse to speak first. Dixon tells us that 'if one person started a speech, the lines would be theirs for that performance' (2016). This strategy must have given the production a semi-improvised quality that perhaps added to its intensity by ensuring that no two performances were the same. Jeremy Herbert's stage design consisted of 'a single large mirror suspended at a 45-degree angle over a plain white floor – visually elegant, but also a metaphor for the script's prism of multiplying personalities' (Dixon 2016). As I noted in this book's introduction, Michael Billington's review provided a reverent, if somewhat reductive account of the performance: 'Judging *4.48 Psychosis* is difficult. How on earth do you award aesthetic points to a 75-minute suicide note? – which is what the play, written shortly before Kane's death, effectively is' (2000). Graham Saunders points out that almost every review of the play's first production used the phrase 'suicide note' (2009, 150). Having unpacked some of its thematic and stylistic features, we are now in a better position to see the limitations of this autobiographical reading of *4.48 Psychosis*. Kane's play is much more than a suicide note, and its artistic value becomes palpably evident in performance.

It wasn't long before European theatre companies produced the work and revealed a range of staging possibilities. Falk Richter directed the play (translated as *4.48 Psychose*) at the *Schaubühne* in Berlin in 2001 and used video projections and music as integral parts of his production. In 2005, Claude Régy staged the play as a two-hander at the *Théâtre des Bouffes du Nord* in Paris. During the latter production, the esteemed film actor Isabelle Huppert performed the text as a quasi-monologue (she occasionally interacted with a therapist figure). Arvind Gaur staged the play as a one-woman show starring the British actress Ruth Sheard in 2005, thereby endorsing Ken Urban's observation that 'the play's multiplicity also creates the uncanny sensation that the text is deeply monologic, the product of a singular, albeit divided, self' (2001, 44). The 2010 TR Warszawa production – first staged in Poland in 2001 and directed by Grzegorz Jarzyna – also functions as a showcase for the virtuosity of a single actor (despite employing several actors). Lyn Gardner described the production in the following terms:'Cielecka is clearly Kane on the last night of her life, angry and desperate yet clinging to life as she confronts her demons, doctors, lovers and even visions of herself as a child and as a future self – a naked, elderly woman' (2010). Gardner also highlights the way the production's design, lighting and soundscape intensify the play's traumatic content and irony. She points out that its industrial soundscape which included 'a crooner singing When I Fall in Love, [served as an] ironic counterpoint to the central character's constant pleas to be loved' (2010). It would be impossible to provide a comprehensive account of all the significant productions of *4.48 Psychosis* within the confines of this short book, and, in any case, I think we learn more about the play by focusing on specific productions in detail. In what follows, I provide an account of two productions of the play. The first tells the intriguing story pf the Belarus Free Theatre' 2005 production in Minsk. The second concentrates on a version produced by Melbourne's Red Stitch Theatre in 2007. The juxtaposition of these productions will highlight the way the play can sustain radically different approaches to the text.

Edward Said once wrote that a written text is the product of 'some immediate contact between author and medium', but once this work is published 'it can be reproduced for the benefit of the world; however much the author demurs at the publicity he receives, once he lets the text go into more than one copy his work is in the world' (1975, 2). Consequently, people read plays like *4.48 Psychosis* according to conditions set by the world. In Said's words, texts are always 'enmeshed in circumstance, time, place and society' (1975, 4). This is not to say that the meaning of a work of art is wholly fixed by material circumstance. However, it is subject to the vicissitudes of worldly change. A postdramatic text like Kane's explicitly embraces this quality of textuality. The salient point here – at least for this chapter – is to underscore the truism that the life of a text is always unpredictable, and subject to reinterpretation as a consequence of a critical or artistic intervention. Just when you think readers have forgotten a once celebrated work, it unexpectedly pops up in a different time, a different place or a different world. Or just when we think we have exhausted a work's interpretive potential or become cynical about its political efficacy, something happens to unsettle our conception of its aesthetic contours and political possibilities.

Belarus Free Theatre (2005 and 2015)

'If theatre can change lives, then, by implication, it can change society, since we're all part of it.'

(Sarah Kane, quoted in Stephenson and Langridge, 1997, 133)

Of all the productions I researched while writing this book, I found the Belarus Free Theatre's staging of the play to be the most compelling. The company generously gave me access to its archival video recordings of both the inaugural 2005 production in Minsk and its restaging in London a decade later. The venue for the first event was a small café called the Graffiti Club, located in the city's industrial area. The tape reveals that the performing space is small and intimate, with the audience in close proximity to the performers. I'd estimate the distance between the back wall and the first row of spectators is about two metres. A ledge runs along the back wall at about chest height, and the area under the shelf is decorated with graffiti. There is a candle burning on the ledge, but most of the light emanates from the café's regular lamps. This is not a purpose-built theatre space – there's no set and no lighting rig. The performance resonates with Grotowski's concept of 'poor theatre' (2002). According to Grotowski, 'theatre can exist without make-up, without autonomic costume and scenography, without a separate performance area (stage), without lighting and sound effects, etc. It cannot exist without the actor–spectator relationship of perceptual, direct, "live" communion' (2002, 19).

Figure 5.1 Belarus Free Theatre, 2005.
Photograph courtesy of Belarus Free Theatre.

Two young women – one blonde, the other brunette – slowly pace back and forth. Then, the blonde woman crouches under the right-hand end of the ledge, while the brunette moves to the candle and picks up a cigarette. The audience is silent, and I can hear the sound of the performers' movements on the recording. They continue to pace up and down the narrow strip of performance space. The blonde woman climbs up and sits on top of the ledge. The brunette sits underneath the ledge, back to the wall, and plays with a cigarette lighter. She has a fag hanging out of her mouth but doesn't light it. The camera pans down, and I can see the floor is littered with white squares. On closer inspection, I can make out that a number is written on each square. The brunette reaches for a packet of cigarettes that are placed next to the candle on the ledge. She takes out some cigarettes and puts them on a black slate on the floor. I can't quite make out what she's doing at first, but then I see that she's laid the cigarettes out to make the numbers '4 48'. The blonde woman joins her on the floor. The blonde takes one of the cigarettes from the slate; the other woman is still playing with the cigarette lighter. The blonde moves towards the lighter and lights her cigarette. This opening sequence lasts for over three minutes and creates a palpable tension that is punctured when the brunette speaks with a slightly maniacal smile on her face, a few seconds after her partner inhales the first drag of the cigarette. And so the play begins. The actors alternate lines, and as the play progresses they look as though they are engaged in some sort of antagonistic dialogue. I can't understand a word they're saying, but I notice there is a deliberate musicality to the way they deliver their lines – sometimes they produce a staccato effect as they speak. As the play progresses, they shriek and holler, whisper and shout. The performance is physical and intense. At times, the performers march up and down the constricted space. At one point, they stuff their mouths with bread as they speak their lines. Towards the end of the play, they produce white balloons, which add a surreal layer to proceedings. The overall effect of this performance is as unsettling as it is mesmerising. Why is this performance significant?

A very convoluted and serendipitous chain of events brought Vladimir Shcherban to Sarah Kane's *4.48 Psychosis*. Shcherban worked for one of the most prestigious theatres in Belarus, the Yanka Kupala National Theatre from the late 1990s. There, he directed a wide range of plays, mostly drawn from the canonical repertoire, by figures such as Goldoni, Shiller and Tennessee Williams. However, Shcherban felt that these works didn't connect with the realities of his life in Belarus. A former Soviet state, Belarus is often described as the world's last dictatorship. Presided over by the so-called 'everlasting president' Alexander Lukashenko, Belarus is a police state. The KGB ensures that the citizens of this small landlocked country live in perpetual fear – the government considers any form of dissenting behaviour tantamount to treason and incarcerates its critics with sinister alacrity. Shcherban's problems began when he became interested in contemporary dramaturgy, and the work of the so-called 'In-Yer-Face' playwrights.

Britain's Royal Court Theatre has run an international playwright's programme for over 20 years, which encourages emerging writers to engage with topical issues and produce provocative drama. In 1999 and 2000, the company ran verbatim theatre workshops in Moscow (Mikhail Ugarov and Elena Gremina established Moscow's Teatr.doc in the wake of these classes). These workshops helped popularise the work of a new generation of British playwrights in Russia. Sometime in 2004, Shcherban discovered the work of Mark Ravenhill through a friend who came back from Moscow and suggested that he read Ravenhill's *Some Explicit Polaroids* (1999). He eventually found what he describes as a 'very bad translation' of Ravenhill's play. Nevertheless, he managed to stage an adaptation at the Belarusian State Theatre where it caused a minor scandal. After receiving a stern caution from the Ministry of Culture, the theatre officials warned Shcherban never to produce a similar work again. The officials were appalled by the play's sexually explicit content, its obscene language and its representation of homosexuality. However, this encounter with Ravenhill's work led him to Sarah Kane's *4.48 Psychosis*. He found a good translation of the play and felt an immediate affinity with it. 'This is exactly what is going on in my head', he told me during an interview in 2017 (2017). Not only did the play resonate with the director's state of mind, but he was able to visualise how he would direct the work immediately. Despite the controversy generated by his production of *Some Explicit Polaroids*, Shcherban decided to stage *4.48 Psychosis* at the Belarusian National Theatre and quickly found two performers – Yana Rusakevich and Olya Shantsina – who were willing to take up the challenge.

Shcherban read the play while he was 'living through a challenging and difficult relationship' and felt that Kane's play accurately captured his mental state. In directing the work, he was trying to find a sound that resonated with Edvard Munch's famous painting *The Scream* (1893). During surreptitious rehearsals held at the National Theatre, the actors screamed loud and often, and their cries carried to a park opposite the theatre building where Minsk's LGBT community regularly gathered. Shcherban recalls that these marginalised people who he identified with were more attuned to the play than some of his 'artistic' colleagues who discouraged him from proceeding with the performance because Belarusians wouldn't 'get' such an experimental work. Despite being locked out of rehearsal studios, and then struggling to find a venue willing to stage the play, Shcherban felt compelled to perform it in front of an audience. It was at this point that he started contacting people outside the world of theatre. Amongst those were Natalia Koliada and Nikolai Khalezin, who organised seminars and writing contests with the hope of encouraging young Belarusians to express their personal and political views through theatre and other artistic mediums. Unfortunately, they were not able to help since they had lost their rented ad-hoc performance space. Koliada and Khalezin did, however, attend the first performance of *4.48 Psychosis* held at the Graffiti Bar. Yana Rusakevich discovered the venue by accident. She spoke to a neighbour about her problem, and he serendipitously happened to be the owner of the bar; he allowed the controversial performance to proceed.

After witnessing the production, Koliada and Khalezin asked Shcherban to join them in their new initiative: the Belarusian Free Theatre (BST), an organisation dedicated to overcoming state censorship. Kane's play became the BST's inaugural production. Since staging *4.48 Psychosis* in May 2005, the Lukashenko regime has arrested and beaten up members of the BST, and Shcherban, Koliada and Khalezin now live in exile. The company, however, currently includes about 50 members, and the BST continue to stage works in Belarus and other parts of the world. Eminent playwrights such as Tom Stoppard and the late Harold Pinter have supported the company's activities, which are a major source of irritation to the Belarusian regime.

Kane's play is not explicitly political, if we define political theatre in a narrow sense – that is, as theatre that addresses explicitly political themes. However, even if we adhere to this conception of political theatre as being concerned with 'political issues', it's possible to argue that *4.48 Psychosis* is political in its caustic critique of the way the UK's National Health system treats people with depression. It also refers to those 'normative' values that make people good, docile citizens, which Kane satirises in her catalogue of 'goals and ambitions': 'to overcome obstacles and attain a high standard/to increase self-regard by the successful exercise of talent' and so on (2001, 233). However, if we take a broader view and define politics as relations of power between different groups in society (Kelleher, 2009, 3), the political force of the play becomes apparent within the context of a country like Belarus. In Belarus, you become an outcast and pariah if you don't conform to a very narrow definition of what constitutes a 'normal' citizen. Shcherban points out that Kane's play unsettles the status quo by addressing topics such as suicide, depression and gender identity. After all, the state doesn't believe that anyone living in Belarus could be depressed, or anything other than heterosexual. According to Shcherban (2017): 'there was no place to start a calm conversation about these issues, it needed to be screamed out, which is why we had to do the play'.

Talking to Shcherban via Skype, I become aware of his passion for the theatre, and his conviction that *4.48 Psychosis* utterly changed his life. Once he read the play, there was no turning back – he simply had to present this work to an audience in Belarus. The story of the relationship between Kane's play and the formation of the BST tells us something about how art may transform people and the often unbearable situations they seek to change. Shcherban and many of his colleagues lost their careers and homes because of their commitment to the BST.

Figure 5.2 Belarus Free Theatre, 2005.
Photograph courtesy of Belarus Free Theatre.

Red Stitch (2007)

I hadn't seen *4.48 Psychosis* on stage until I saw Melbourne's
Red Stitch Company's production of the play in 2007. At
the time, I was rehearsing the student production of the
play I described in the last chapter. I was so impressed by
this work that I immediately questioned my approach to the
text, which seemed so ham-fisted and gauche in contrast
to the tightly focused and beautifully performed version
I had just witnessed. Red Stitch is an independent theatre
company located in Melbourne and run by a collective of
actors who specialise in producing contemporary theatre
works rarely seen in Australia. Alyson Campbell directed

the Red Stitch production of Kane's play, and it was mesmerising, elegant and strangely moving for a performance
that avoided overt displays of emotion. Campbell paid close
attention to Kane's language, which her four actors intoned
in a variety of ways. They sometimes spoke in unison, and
their trained voices produced a choral musicality, which
served to heighten the meaning of the lines. Sometimes
a single line was distributed among the cast, which created a staccato effect that conveyed the sense of language
and meaning breaking down altogether. Each actor also
recited large slabs of the text with a great deal of emotional
restraint. On these occasions, they delivered their lines like
a conventional dramatic monologue. They also played the
pauses to great effect.

On entering the space, the audience encountered the four
actors standing still on a minimal set, bathed in hues of sky
blue and glacial white, covered in what looked like abundant
quantities of fake snowflakes. The performance space looked
like the living room of a house stripped bare of creature com-
forts, and there were a series of receding doorways behind the
actors, creating the impression of entrapment in a labyrinth.
The actors held their stillness long after the audience had
settled in their seats. This strategy gave the spectators ample
time to contemplate the tableau while also respecting the
text's first stage direction. When the actors spoke, the effect of
breaking the silence was almost shocking. Campbell did not
attempt to distribute the lines of the play among recognisable characters. Instead, the actors performed as though they
were part of a single, fragmented consciousness. I later discovered Campbell used what we might call a 'post-humanist'
approach to the play to avoid creating recognisable characters
(see Waddington, 2010).

Figure 5.3 Red Stitch Theatre's Production of *4.48 Psychosis* directed by Alyson Campbell.
Photograph by Jodie Hutchinson.

The production's greatest strength was the way Campbell and her actors paid close attention to Kane's language. They delivered their lines with precision and clarity, which underscored certain nuances in the text – nuances I hadn't noticed when I read the play. They also gave the lines a sense of physical dynamism by alternating a 'stand-and-deliver' approach with a series of choreographed, almost dance-like moves, which produced numerous permutations of the actors' spatial arrangement on the stage. The overall effect was quite stunning, and the image of the performers in a cold labyrinth, literally covered in snow, functioned as an apt metaphor for despair – the performers appeared to be trapped in an unrelenting winter world. The title of Kane's play echoes an incident in

C. S. Lewis' novel *The Silver Chair* (1953), which is part of the Narnia series, and set in a world of everlasting winter. The prince in the novel experiences an hour of sanity each night, which the other characters see as an instance of madness (see Diedrich, 2013, 384). Campbell found Kane's references to *The Silver Chair* extremely suggestive. She was keen to explore 'the idea of a spell cast that leads one to believe in the "truth" of one [version of] reality, but being released for an hour every night to "remember" that it is not real' (quoted in D'Cruz, 2010, 110).

Campbell – who is a Kane scholar as well as a theatre director – was initially attracted to Kane's writing by the challenge posed by the 'openness' of the text (an 'openness' shared by postdramatic writing for the theatre). She wanted to avoid the impression that there is a single consciousness at the heart of the text. With this in mind, Campbell rejected what she called the 'victim, perpetrator, bystander' logic of the Royal Court production. She also deliberately avoided creating any doctor/patient dialogue between the performers. However, she did commission a sound designer to support the actors' voices, and to intensify the impression that the stage represented an interior world cut off from all external referents: 'I wanted to create a world that was experienced for itself and then affects how we re-enter the world beyond the stage' (quoted in D'Cruz 2010, 110). The cool, resigned atmosphere of this production contrasts sharply with the impassioned, aggressive volume of the Belarus productions. I found it fascinating to see such disparate interpretations of the same text – and it's important to stress the fact that I don't consider one better than the other. Rather, they both reinforce Kane's belief that her apparently 'enigmatic' text shines in performance (Dixon, 2016).

References

Artaud, Antonin (1958) *The Theatre and Its Double*. Translated by Mary Caroline Richards. New York: Grove Press.

Billington, Michael (2001) 'How Do You Judge a 75-minute Suicide Note?' *The Guardian* www.theguardian.com/stage/2000/jun/30/theatre.artsfeatures. Accessed 27 July 2017.

Carter, Paul (2004) *Material Thinking*. Melbourne: Melbourne University Publishing.

D'Cruz, Glenn (2010) Teaching/Directing *4.48 Psychosis*. *Australasian Drama Studies* 57: 99–114.

Diedrich, Antje. (2013) 'Last in a Long Line of Literary Kleptomaniacs': Intertextuality in Sarah Kane's *4.48 Psychosis*. *Modern Drama* 56:3: 374–398.

Dixon, Andrew (2016) '"The Strange Thing is we Howled with Laughter": Sarah Kane's enigmatic last play'. *The Guardian* www.theguardian.com/stage/2016/may/11/448-psychosis-sarah-kane-new-opera-philip-venables-royal-opera-house. Accessed 28 July 2017.

Gardner, Lyn (2010) '4.48 Psychosis'. *The Guardian* www.theguardian.com/stage/2010/mar/26/448-psychosis-review. Accessed 28 July 2017.

Grotowski, Jerzy (2002) *Towards a Poor Theatre*. Ed. Eugenio Barba. London and New York: Routledge.

Kane, Sarah (2001) *Complete Plays*. Ed. David Greig London: Methuen.

Kelleher, Joe (2009) *Theatre and Politics*. London: Palgrave.

Lewis, C. S. (1953) *The Silver Chair*. New York: Harper Collins.

Ravenhill, Mark (1999) *Some Explicit Polaroids*. London: Methuen.

Said, Edward, W. (1975) 'The Text, the World, the Critic'. *The Bulletin of the Midwest Modern Language Association* 8:2: 1–23.

Saunders, Graham (2009) *About Kane: the Playwright and the Work*. London: Faber and Faber.

Shcherban, Vladimir (2017) Personal Interview with Glenn D'Cruz, 7 April 2017.

Stephenson, Heidi and Langridge, Natasha (1997) *Rage and Reason: Women Playwrights on Playwriting*. London: Methuen.

Urban, Ken (2001) '"An Ethics of Catastrophe": The Theatre of Sarah Kane'. *Performing Arts Journal* 69: 36–46.

Waddington, Julie. (2010) 'Posthumanist Identities in Sarah Kane', *Sarah Kane in Context*. Ed. Laurens de Vos and Graham Saunders. Manchester: Manchester University Press: 139–148.

Conclusion

I began this book by claiming that *4.48 Psychosis* is a play shrouded in mythology, and argued that Sarah Kane's untimely suicide casts a prurient shadow over her dramatic oeuvre. This tragic event makes it difficult to appreciate her work on its own terms. During a discussion following the Belarus Free Theatre's restaging of *4.48 Psychosis* in London in 2015, Dominic Dromgoole, the celebrated British theatre director and one of Kane's close friends, tells the audience that Kane was a person of 'enormous joy' and 'great fun' (2015). Apparently, she loved parties and had an infantile sense of humour, qualities sadly masked by her posthumous reputation.

However, as I argued in Chapter 2, her illness *coincides* with her play but is not reducible to her suffering, and subsequent suicide. The fact that so many artists (and teachers) continue to reinterpret the play in performance testifies to Kane's shrewd theatrical imagination. The work, like many postdramatic scripts, invites theatre practitioners to radically interpret the text in performance, which is why *4.48 Psychosis* burns brightest on the stage, and the play continues to stimulate a welter of activity: from scholarly readings and theorisations of the text to educational and professional performances all over the world. In short, *4.48 Psychosis* continues to lead a full life almost 20 years after the death of its author.

That said, it's important not to forget that Kane wrote about an experience she knew all too well, and the play, even when read on the page, has a ring of truth about it. Whether you interpret the play as a critique of the medical profession's pharmacological approach to treating mental illness, or as work that identifies love, and perhaps even gender confusion as the source of despair, *4.48 Psychosis* resonates with people because it captures the anxious tenor of the contemporary world. Life on planet earth has never been so precarious for so many people, even those ensconced in relatively affluent parts of the world. The apocalyptic threat of climate change and the rapid spread of surveillance technologies, coupled with widespread economic inequality, and the threat of international terrorism has increased human despair exponentially. Today, intolerant political and religious movements aggressively persecute people for being different and provide yet another source of existential anxiety for outliers and pariahs. The self is under siege, and a lot of people have good reason to dissolve under pressure to conform and consume. Some even feel guilty for not following the imperative to enjoy life. Kane once remarked that turning one's sense of hopelessness and anguish into art is 'the most hopeful and life-affirming thing a person can do' (quoted in Saunders, 2009, 105). I hope this book demonstrates that *4.48 Psychosis* deserves our attention and admiration because Sarah Kane created something beautiful out of despair, something that continues to inspire people to exercise their creativity and rage against the dying of the light.

References

Dromgoole, Dominic (2015) Belarus Free Theatre Video (private archive).

Saunders, Graham (2009) *About Kane: the Playwright and the Work*. London: Faber and Faber.

Index